Heart Prayers

Heart Prayers

A Life Restored after Decades of Abuse

CINDY REUST

WESTBOW
PRESS®
A DIVISION OF THOMAS NELSON
& ZONDERVAN

This book is a work of non-fiction. Unless otherwise noted, the author
and the publisher make no explicit guarantees as to the accuracy of
the information contained in this book and in some cases, names
of people and places have been altered to protect their privacy.

WestBow Press books may be ordered through booksellers or by contacting:

WestBow Press
A Division of Thomas Nelson & Zondervan
1663 Liberty Drive
Bloomington, IN 47403
www.westbowpress.com
844-714-3454

Scripture taken from the New King James Version®. Copyright © 1982
by Thomas Nelson. Used by permission. All rights reserved.

ISBN: 978-1-6642-2161-1 (sc)
ISBN: 978-1-6642-2160-4 (hc)
ISBN: 978-1-6642-2162-8 (e)

Library of Congress Control Number: 2021901659

Print information available on the last page.

WestBow Press rev. date: 02/03/2021

꧁꧂

*To my precious sister Victoria (1948–2019), who suffered
most of her life and found hope and eternal healing in
the loving arms of her Lord and Savior Jesus!*

꧁꧂

Acknowledgments

As the Lord spoke to me of the endeavor of this book, it rested heavily on my heart. I believe his wishes were that my writing reflects brief accounts of my past abuse and his faithful restoration. I felt overwhelmed as obedience to his call pounded my not-measuring-up button. I believed he asked more of me than I could deliver, and I was right. But he was not asking more than he and I together could deliver.

My past includes recovery from many different forms of sexual and emotional abuse and the traumatic experiences of numerous betrayals, which I felt at the beginning of this project that I was, for the most part, highly or at least higher functioning than I was decades before. I was unprepared for the healing that he would do as he asked me to go deeper and deeper into my emotions, producing a greater level of transparency.

God has delivered me from a very dark place filled with anxiety and the fear of literally everything. I was afraid of everything and trusted nothing! In the middle of my recovery, he placed in my heart a burden for those, like myself, who had lived their lives on life's bloody battlefield and were also trying to survive and recover from one incident to the next.

I am praying for God's very best as you read, and if you haven't already embarked on the journey of wholeness God desires for you, I pray that you will invite him in to set up his kingdom in your heart.

Along with the many holy benefits I have already shared, I had the added blessing on this journey of my sister Ruth's faithful prayers, editing, encouragement, words of truth, and accountability that comes from being the oldest. Thank you, Sis! I believe God intended for you and me to share this journey.

Dear Reader,

In the pages ahead, you might notice that each prayer skips the greeting and moves directly into conversation. The reason for this is that the Lord has impressed on my heart and unfolded into my daily walk the importance of remaining continually in his presence. To abide with our Creator is our highest privilege.

It is my prayer that as you begin to read of my trials and victories, you would find hope for all that has prevented you from walking in the fullness of our precious Lord. Blessings on your journey!

In Christ, who is our source,

Cindy

*H*umanity discovered me early! Dark, deviant humanity opened my innocent eyes to the inconceivable potential of people. I searched for a refuge, convinced I was alone in my valley and without hope. Tired and defeated from the enduring battle, I at last found the rest I had hoped for. The Spirit of God revealed his faithful presence in the valley.

As I walked, filled with new hope, I was able to see that the Lord had always been with me, adjusting my path and protecting me from the battles that were not part of his purpose or plan for my life.

He continues to walk with me as he heals my soul and molds and shapes my character, preparing me for such a time as this, a moment to share with others that they are not alone in their valley.

"O God the Lord, the strength of my salvation, You have covered my head in the day of battle" (*Psalm 140:7*).

*I*t is my heart's desire that my life should be made over to reflect your love and compassion. I pray daily that you will use me to further your kingdom. Lord, you have changed my life. You have been faithful to hear my cry and rescue me from my fears, restoring peace to my life. I desire to bring honor and glory to your name through my every action, thought, and deed. Amen!

"He will fulfill the desire of those who fear Him; He also will hear their cry and save them" (Psalm 145:19).

*E*quipped only with senses that were knocked out of scope as a child, I lacked the breadth and depth of understanding to look beyond the betrayals that framed my young life. I had a naturally developing understanding that trust was treachery in the making. I adapted within my own character a need to become my own safe refuge. Little did I know, I was a house built out of straw, frail to the impending elements. It wasn't long before my house and resolve were broken and lying flat on the ground.

From under the straw and rubble, you heard my sobs for the hope of a deliverer to usher me to the warmth of the utopia of my dreams. In my weakness, I accepted the outstretched hand, with no questions asked. Slowly and consistently, you opened my eyes to the truth of the utopia that awaits me in the new spirit that has come to dwell within me. I have found strength through my weakness and love through my willingness to take your hand. My house is built on solid rock, and it will not fall!

"Bow down Your ear to me, Deliver me speedily;
Be my rock of refuge, A fortress of defense to save
me" (Psalm 31:2).

imes too numerous to count, you have intercepted my mind from the deep well of anxiety through tender reflections of your abounding goodness and promises to protect me. You still my racing heart by placing a song in it. Father, you are the one true remedy for fear. With thanksgiving in my heart, I give thanks for your peace, which surpasses all of my human understanding.

"For you have been a shelter for me, A strong tower from the enemy" (Psalm 61:3).

*M*y earliest memories are rooted in the ever-changing unknown of circumstances beyond my control. This foundation of confusion cultivated a fear of everything, including you, Lord. Because I was afraid of you, that fear fertilized the belief that you held enmity toward me.

What do people do when they believe the one who created them does not love or accept them? I ran wildly and wandered the wasteland, searching for a love to replace the one I felt you were withholding. My search took me on a trek that spanned many years with even more painful disappointments before I found you waiting for me at the bottom of myself.

The whole time I was searching, I believe you were waiting with a resilient love for me to become still enough to hear the sound of your voice, calling me into the security and love of your arms.

"For as the heavens are high above the earth, So great is His mercy toward those who fear him" (Psalm 103:11).

*T*hank you for reminding me that I am uniquely made with a divine purpose. No matter what my strengths or weaknesses are, I am righteous in your sight, having been received into holiness through the precious blood of Jesus Christ. My wounds are no longer welcome guests in this temple created by your hand!

I have been made new, and through the rebirth of my spirit, I long to live in your presence, growing, thriving, and in all ways honoring your complete sacrifice for my life.

———————

"Blessed is he who considers the poor; The LORD will deliver him in time of trouble" (Psalm 41:1).

For me, the lapse of time grew through the years, like chapters of a whodunit novel where the ending hung in the distance just beyond my reach. The suspenseful theme read like an infusion of robbery, which over time and through the continuum of theft began to transform my once-naïve innocence into a dark soul filled with fear, anxiety, shame, and incomprehensible doubt!

Father, asking for your help with the hard questions allowed me to receive the hard answers, which you faithfully used to bring the truth into my life. I am so grateful that you have written the sequel to my story in the Book of Life.

You have filled my heart with the truth of your story, and it has removed the lies that had once bonded shame and doubt to my soul. Because of your story, my story finally has an ending—one of confidence in the eternal love of my Creator!

"He has made His wonderful works to be remembered; The Lord is gracious and full of compassion" (Psalm 111:4).

ou have freed me from my burdens. Because of your mercy, my load is light. In the storms that rise to claim victory over my life, you are my safe harbor. Without you, I am tossed freely; my existence depends on your guidance and protection. You are my rock, and in your presence, there is only unconditional love.

———————

"He shall cry to Me, You are my Father, My God, and the rock of my salvation" (Psalm 89:26).

The deepest part of who I am was at one point afraid to trust in a God whom I felt had allowed unthinkable things to happen to me. Filled with confusion and resentment, I built walls to protect myself from the world and insulate my heart from witnessing the profound love you had for others when I felt utterly forsaken.

Father, I am so grateful that you helped me to see that my experiences created injuries that not only left a scab over my heart but also created a blindness to your love and compassion, both of which are my eternal inheritance.

I walked alone in my pain out of my blindness and not the disregard I believed you felt for me. You have faithfully breathed new life into my being, lifting me from glory to glory. Every breath I have taken is a living testament to the sanctifying love that flows from the cross.

"For Your mercy reaches unto the heavens, And Your truth unto the clouds" (Psalm 57:10).

*Y*our acts of love know no limits. Just a whisper from your child and you offer floodgates of life-changing blessings. Salvation is the supreme act of love that you offer freely to those who choose to worship only you.

Who of their own free will would choose to wander aimlessly in darkness over experiencing the eternal life and unconditional love that is offered to all who in faith call your name?

"Return, O Lord, deliver me! Oh, save me for Your mercies sake!" (Psalm 6:4).

I never doubted that I was in your sight, but I would never have described the way I felt as precious. I remember the moments beyond number where my soul cowered with the fear of eternal rejection as I daily felt beat to the ground, envisioning a holy glare descending from the throne. The hatred that I believed you felt toward me only confirmed and gave life to the loathing I felt for myself.

I long for the day to throw myself at your feet in eternal gratitude for renewing my mind with the truth as you patiently walk with me through the very long process of acknowledging the lies of the enemy and then replacing them with truth and the holy legitimacy that while I am a sinner, I am worthy of love!

———————

"He will redeem their life from oppression and violence; And precious shall be their blood in His sight" (Psalm 72:14).

hrough your undying love, I am transformed into a child healed by your grace and filled with your peace. Daily you make it possible for me to experience your true nature. Your love quenches past hurts and brings new life where fear and anxiety once lived. Because of your guiding touch, I am able to put the past behind and learn to trust in your devotion as my Father and my Lord.

"Many sorrows shall be to the wicked; But he who trusts in the Lord, mercy shall surround him" (*Psalm 32:10*).

The reality of my options for help was exhausted, having found no one with the holy keys to unlock the sickness inside my soul, a sickness that had entirely blocked out the truth that I am a child of God and through his love for me, I had the unlimited resources of the Holy Spirit!

Your endless love is the divine trademark of your character and the seal on the restored life I am eternally blessed to embrace in service for you.

In all things, I now see the sovereign touch of an eternity of planning. Forgive me for ever believing my life's hardships, no matter how great, were bigger than the One who created in love, the air I breathe.

"I love the LORD, because He has heard My voice and my supplications" (Psalm 116:1).

se me, Lord, to comfort others through the storms that I might, even in the smallest way, offer the hope of safe passage to your abundant grace. Your deep and abiding love is the greatest gift I can share with others. Let my life be a reflection that peace only exists where Jesus lives!

"As for God, His way is perfect; The word of the LORD is proven; He is a shield to all who trust in Him" (Psalm 18:30).

You have been my hope, the unknown longing of my heart, and mercifully the champion who has saved me from death. In my desperate search for love, I found hearts made filthy by the world, and I paid the price with pieces of my soul. I sought that which didn't exist, the pure and uncontaminated gift of love and acceptance! All the while, you, the Almighty, had already paid the price for my life with the pure sacrifice of the Righteous Lamb!

With each day, my mind is becoming clearer to the holy significance of sacrifice and the symbolic weight of the cross. Substituting my sin for the Lamb's life was an atonement that seems only to rival the love it took to bear the world's sin on your body. Your sacrifice is a holy standard and model for which I am daily grateful to embrace. The redemptive power of your unwavering love has been the source of my passion, and I pray that you would be glorified in my life.

"For He has delivered me out of all trouble; And my eye has seen its desire upon my enemies" (Psalm 54:7).

When fears grip me, you are faithful to relieve my suffering. I have come to trust in your name as my lifeline to peace of mind, body, and spirit. You are the Creator of everything, and I know that you will always provide me a way to stand up under the weight of my burdens, no matter how significant.

"Our help is in the name of the LORD, Who made heaven and earth" (Psalm 124:8).

Father, many times I felt the Holy Spirit's gentle tug of conviction and recognized a critical and judgmental behavior seeping up from my depth, or not so deep, place in my soul. Why is it that in my sometimes inability to see myself as the righteous bride of Christ, I attempt instead the fruitless prospect of puffing myself up by focusing on the shortcomings I see in myself and the world? This leaves me feeling a sense of shame and despair as I try to reengage with a now-diminished light, limiting how others can see you in me.

Thank you, Lord, for teaching me how measuring success can define our station in life, by worldly standards of course. By kingdom standards, great success is not measured by achievement, but by service to you with a fully surrendered heart.

The greatest hill I have had to climb is Mt. Shame with a sweeping vista of my life from Pride Point. Comparing my worth, value, past, present, and even future with the world, in an attempt to even out and shamefully, at times, elevate my own self-appreciation at the expense of judging was a stronghold the enemy used to block the freedom I inherited at the cross.

Forgive me, Father, for judging the world that I am commissioned to love and for self-assessing my value or worth by pre-cross principles. You are faithful to remind me that my light comes not from what I have or can accomplish, but for what I have surrendered.

"Save now, I pray, O LORD; O LORD, I pray, send now prosperity" (Psalm 118:25).

My worth comes from the precious value you have placed on me. I am so thankful that you are faithful and committed to restoring my life. I desire to serve you with a heart of gratitude and a spirit of submission.

Heavenly Father, as you continue to watch over me, I pray for truth to forge a deep vein of faith between us. I am of your flock and dependent on your care. Your continual shepherding gives my life security and the peace to walk in purpose and meaning.

"The LORD shall preserve your going out and your coming in From this time forth, and even forevermore" (Psalm 121:8).

I remember a time when I felt certain that suffering embodied whom I was, from my nucleus to the freckles on my checks. I didn't draw a breath, which hadn't felt like its origin began with the shame and guilt resulting from the theft of my purity. By my estimation, I had not breathed an unrestricted mouthful of air, filled with life-absorbing peace, in my existence.

Father, you saw me facedown in the emotion-stained dirt at the bottom of the pit long before I cried out to be rescued. You know the whole unrevised story of how I went from the safety of the womb to the end of life as I knew it at the bottom of that deep, dark hole.

I am so grateful that you were unconcerned with the how and why of where you found me and which portion I was to blame. You met me in my desperate need, and in your mercy, you began pulling me from the darkness into the light of truth. Step by scary step, your faithful and tender renewal of all that I was filled my heart with a new and pure love that has restored my hope and redeemed with certainty that you are my Father and I am loved. Help me to take every thought captive unto complete obedience to you.

"I called on the Lᴏʀᴅ in distress; The Lᴏʀᴅ answered me and set me in a broad place" (Psalm 118:5).

With holy invention, I was woven together. Every detail was under your inspired watch, as the originality of your power and love unfolded into the creation of me.

Inconceivable to my mind are the capacities of your mighty touch. There has never been or will there ever be another who compares to you, Father.

I am praising your faithfulness, as the works of your spirit are again molding, shaping, and rooting out the fear and anxiety left behind by the less than holy works of others. Perfect is your plan for holy restoration, for those who fix their eyes on the Good Shepherd.

"My frame was not hidden from You, When I was made in secret, And skillfully wrought in the lowest parts of the earth" (Psalm 139:15).

alking in the light of the one true God has been a daily encounter of the transforming power that began to happen in my life once I allowed my heart to trust you. This became easier as my faith grew, as did my ability to surrender without fear of betrayal.

At times I felt I was seeing my past scroll across the marquee of my mind. As this happened, something told me I was watching the cast in this particular dramatic performance take the lead in my life for the last time!

Thank you, Father, for every single life-changing collision of consciousness, as you have ushered in healing and the redemptive exchange of your life for mine.

> "Blessed are the people who know the joyful sound! They walk, O Lord, in the light of Your countenance" (Psalm 89:15).

*I*n reflecting, so many memories are released into that formerly brittle place in my awareness. Vivid is the tender fears that once led me to the edge of reason, altering the course of my life and forever more sending me on a journey in pursuit of truth, healing, hope, and all things that are life-restoring.

I am convinced that I am alive today because of your enduring love, which stood by me through every crisis, every racing heart and teeth-chattering episode. Every tear-stained pillow led me that much closer to you and a love that refused to let go. I believe I stand as a living example that the prevailing stamina of the all-loving God is infinitely real and available to anyone who would believe and then receive the life-renewing hope that is found only in relationship with you!

"Oh, give thanks to the LORD, for He is good! For His mercy endures forever" (Psalm 118:29).

While growing up insulated, the outside world became, to me, a place that seemed confusing and unsafe. As I grew up, isolation became a normal way of life. I was lonely, but I felt safe. The trade-off seemed to make good survival sense, but in truth it was a manufactured lie from God's competition.

The enemy wanted me to believe that if I exposed myself to the world, I was unprotected. God did not alter the free will of my abusers; nor is he responsible for my wounds. Yet in his mercy and profound love, he has walked through every pain-filled memory and healed every scar.

Father, you opened my eyes to the fraud of the enemy and showered truth in my once-narrow scope of reality. In the remoteness of my life, I didn't realize there was a real battle being fought for my spirit. I believed life was life and heaven was heaven. Thank you for rescuing me from the deceiver's attacks and for showing me that Jesus is the eternal bridge that has led me from death to life.

"Hear my prayer, O Lord, Give ear to my supplications! In Your faithfulness answer me, And in Your righteousness" (Psalm 143:1).

Throughout my earthly safari, I have many times encountered the darkness of man's heart and the depth of his selfishness. I have been nearly mortally wounded by the conduct of those with whom my heart had been intimately linked. In my suffering, I thought they to be the worst of your creation. The enormity of pain it must have required to reach a point of utter disregard for another human brings new sorrow to a place in my heart that once only held anger.

Father, you have reached into my ailing soul and unraveled old mysteries too painful to explore, and with flawless timing, you placed each incident under the glass to be examined through discernment that only you could ordain. I am forever grateful for the yoke that is no longer mine to carry. The grace you have given me in my time of need has forever changed my power when responding to the enemy's attempts to reclaim what is now yours for all of eternity!

"Great is the LORD, and greatly to be praised; And His greatness is unsearchable" (Psalm 145:3).

*Y*ou are resolute in your love, and unwavering has been the sustaining yet silent grip on my life regardless of the paths I have chosen. Whether sunshine or storms, my life has always been under sovereign observation.

You have taught me a new standard of truth. My feelings have lied and deceived me during the worst of circumstances, for which you have faithfully delivered me. By your grace, fear or emotion no longer govern my decisions. Your truth has set me free!

———

"For great is Your mercy toward me, And You have delivered my soul from the depths of Sheol" (Psalm 86:13).

With awesome wonder, I look within to embrace the jewel of God's precious Holy Spirit! In love and gentleness, he continually nudges and whispers me into a fullness of heart and mind I never imagined possible.

Without his presence, I would have remained forever tossed about in the perpetual hell of spiritual and emotional brokenness. I long to embrace new attributes and to share the glory of the new fruit in my life, as it gives birth to the discovery of the wellspring of purpose absent in my life until now.

Father, give me ears to hear and eyes to see the divine teaching, and let my mind be open and hungry for the sanctification that only you can do.

———

> "By awesome deeds in righteousness You will answer us, O God of our salvation, You who are the confidence of all the ends of the earth, And of the far-off seas" (Psalm 65:5).

My need to hear your voice has never been stronger than at the crossroads of life. Whether the shift has been emotional, relational, or life-calling, the need for deity-inspired decision-making causes me to press in until the quietest of holy whispers hits my ear like the roar of the incoming tide.

Help me to leave my flesh and the fears and idols that accompany them forever at the altar. Enable me to leave my cares behind, as together we walk in the quiet of the garden, as you teach me of the beauty that awaits a surrendered life. I trust you, Lord, to work all things out according to your will. Your perfect love is a gift to be treasured!

"For You are my rock and my fortress; Therefore, for Your name's sake, Lead me and guide me" (Psalm 31:3).

My worldly vices were gratifying in ways that were difficult for me to understand and even more so to express to you, except to say I always felt a sense of primal satisfaction as I partook in my vice, that is, until immediately following the successful collaboration between the enemy, the vice, and my flesh. The veil of shame would promptly flow across me with a knee-buckling intensity as the weight of the emotional stronghold was too much to repeatedly endure.

I wanted to escape the hollow emptiness that echoed still louder through my soul with each new dishonoring reminder of my having chosen the proverbial apple rather than connection with you.

Help me to remember that you are a God who loves without limits, not one who shames or condemns. Your love has cast fear and anxiety far from me, changing the course of my tomorrows forever.

"Then they cried out to the Lord in their trouble, And He saved them out of their distresses" (Psalm 107:19)

*M*y soul yearned for your company long before you began to penetrate the hardened blindness that existed in my heart. You gave life to the still-bleeding wounds, allowing them to become transparent to me.

Fear and resentment had echoed through my soul, like voices feeding back from the depth of a cavern. All I could hear was the sound of my own need to be validated without surrender and the freedom to resent to the fullest measure of my being, without shouldering the spiritual impact of hate. I demanded fairness yet was blind to my own sin.

You have faithfully walked me through the grief, helping me to discover the price for resentment is a debt already paid for an ungrateful heart. Thank you, Father, for lifting the veil and exposing me to the sins of my own soul.

You have faithfully walked with me through the deposits left behind in the minefield of my character and have carefully removed their power to harm. In love, you have forever bore the weight of my sins and those committed against me.

In all ways I am a new creation and praising eternally the name of Jesus!

"My soul waits for the Lord More than those who watch for the morning—Yes, more than those who watch for the morning" (Psalm 130:6).

You established through the cross that your grace is greater than the sum of my substantial sins. Not capable of repaying my debt, you willing became my Lamb in an outpouring of love incomparable in time since or beyond.

You have shown me both mercy and grace through your sacrifice. You have delivered me from my enemies, you have redeemed me, and you have healed my mind from painful and intrusive thoughts, but greatest of all, you have loved me unconditionally. I want for nothing except more of you!

———

"And have not shut me up into the hand of the enemy; You have set my feet in a wide place" (Psalm 31:8).

When anxiety begins to surface, my fears surround me, filling my mind with the familiar impending doom. In that dark moment, I hear the voice of your Spirit within me, reminding me that I am not alone.

As I am afraid yet secure in your loving care, minute by minute, the isolation fades, and I feel my victory begin to emerge. I know my promised peace is near. I will never experience a greater strength in my weakness or a deeper love apart from you, Father.

As you drive back the enemy's attempts to trap me in the past, by tearing down his stronghold, I seek your face with a grateful heart. I praise your name and give thanks for the victories that await me today as your child.

"In the multitude of my anxieties within me, Your comforts delight my soul" (Psalm 94:19).

*L*ord, in this moment, let not your promises elude me as my mind rehearses the what-ifs while guilt and shame cast shadows, stealing my hope of sleep. My soul wants so badly to rest on the hilltop. It is not to be as the enemy lays claim again to the slumber that is rightly mine.

As I await the sleep that seems to never come, I am softly reminded by the one who knit me together to close my eyes and meditate on the truth of his faithful love, whose blessings and provision never cease. You tenderly shower my thoughts with your peace, and soon the battle that was already won on the cross becomes the cradle to which I find rest and slumber.

Lord, with a heart full of hymns, you tuck me within the shelter of your wing. It has never been too full for me. Your love is my rock; your grace is my fortress. Lord, thank you for restoring strength to your battle-weary child.

"I will both lie down in peace, and sleep; For You alone, O LORD, make me dwell in safety" (Psalm 4:8).

When the storm comes, bringing with it fragmented memories swirling through my mind, like a cyclone full of daggers, my heart races, taking captive my thoughts. It is your love and promise of protection that I cling to. You are my only hope!

In the shelter of your wing, you shower my fears with your grace and truth, and in love, your spirit begins to sore within me. Thank you for the promise of being one with the sound of my voice. This assurance has restored my peace. Blessed be the name of the Lord!

"Preserve me, O God, for in You I put my trust" (Psalm 16:1).

When my mind begins to race with that familiar pattern and my thinking begins to harness the energy from fearful thoughts, which the longtime trauma of painful past experiences ignited, I know that in the midst of that dark moment, you are within me, encouraging me to reach within myself to claim your promise of a sound mind.

It is through your amazing love that peace flows through my soul, and hope is again restored, as I step into my promised healing and know that I am safe.

"In the day of my trouble I will call upon You, For You will answer me" (Psalm 86:7).

Guide me down the path of righteousness for it is only through the surrender of laying down my life and following you that my life will bear fruit. As I meditate both day and night on you, let your spirit bring peace to my soul and healing to my heart. Let my every action, thought, and deed bring glory and honor to you, my King.

I know it is your will that my life has been restored. You have healed the soul wounds that had once robbed me of the precious intimacy my heart desired. Glory to you for the renewing of my mind as you have filled my thoughts with the eternal grace and beauty that flows freely from your love. Let it be your will alone that guides my path and sustains me throughout my day.

"Let the words of my mouth and the meditation of my heart be acceptable in Your sight, O Lord, my strength and my Redeemer" (Psalm 19:14).

Father, it's incredible to me how blind I was to the emotional gravity in my life as it pulled me in almost-sensible ways onto the collision course of others who, like myself, carried profound injuries in very distinct places. Forgive me for embracing my soul and allowing myself to be led in perfect cadence toward the male counterpart of my own destructive and rebellious patterns.

I will forever praise your name for the redemptive power of your healing love, as you cleared away the confusion that allowed me to initially see the false refuges of my past as gifts. My flesh screamed for more until thankfully my soul became so sick from being consumed by this illusion of acceptance, each time mistaking it for love.

For me, this created a crisis of what was real. The tangible impact proved to be the gateway to recovery from the addiction and dependency, the gods I served. You are my refuge and my hope, and only in you will I place my trust!

"You are my hiding place and my shield; I hope in Your word" (Psalm 119:114).

My heart, once filled with unrelenting sadness, is now a place where the joy of my Lord fuels my soul with new hope and the triumphs wait for me with every new day.

No longer do I awaken to foreboding condemnation playing daily encore performances to the tempo of my alarm clock. My peace comes only from you, Father, as I rest in the confidence of your loving protection. You have ushered me through the shadow of death and on to green pastures, where you continue to restore within me that which falls short of your perfect and desired outcome.

Because of you, my heart is full of the expectancy of daily encounters with the greatest friend I have ever known. My Redeemer lives!

"But I will sing of Your power; Yes, I will sing aloud of Your mercy in the morning; For You have been my defense and refuge in the day of my trouble" (Psalm 59:16).

*T*he healing miracles you have worked in my life have changed my outlook on the way I now view my past as well as my hope for my tomorrows.

Because of the hope you have given me through your unrelenting compassion, I aspire to see the world around me through the possibilities and no longer by my history. You have embraced me, and I have discovered the eternal treasure of fellowship with you as I thrive, soaring to new heights, becoming all I was created to be as a child of the King of Kings.

"You are the God who does wonders; You have declared Your strength among the peoples" (Psalm 77:14).

My wounds, once beating with the pulse of sorrow, have now become a place of fertile soil, offering perhaps hope and encouragement to others. Joyous is my heart as the recipient of your mercy and grace.

I am abundantly blessed to be walking in the glory of a life delivered from the abuse that drove a wedge of separation between your love and my eternal need.

Father, until recently, I hadn't given much consideration to the power of sanctification. I now feel as if, by your hands, I have been hammered, pounded, and heated again and again and again! Until only then, the beauty of the gold has finally begun to surface from the ashes, shining, whole, and in the image of the Master, who has created within me a unique nature molded especially by his love and for his good purpose.

"While I live I will praise the LORD; I will sing praises to my God while I have my being" (Psalm 146:2).

Since the moment I recognized you as my Creator and acknowledged you as my Lord, you have faithfully been my guide through the sweetest of valleys and storms so severe I felt crushed beneath the emotional fallout.

Most of my life I felt the sting of the tightrope beneath my feet, as I used every resource I possessed to keep from plummeting to a darkness unknown to me. You held back the winds, stabilizing my crossing and keeping me from harm as I sought with incredible fear and reservation the God of the Bible.

You came alive to me, and in learning of whom you are for the first time, I found myself, my purpose, and my passions. I am eternally grateful!

"You enlarged my path under me, So my feet did not slip" (Psalm 18:36).

I have come to learn the trap that was set for me was carefully arranged long before I took up residency in my mother's womb. The strategy of the enemy's trap thrived as my flesh gave way to rebellion and the cultivated weakness that God's holy armor was designed to defeat.

The enemy's careful planning was successful as he ushered in years of trauma and abuse, leaving in their wake strongholds of fear and insecurity in the world around me, but especially in you, my Savior.

I was like a terrified bird in a cage, but you tried repeatedly to open the door and free me. Yet I lacked the courage to trust you, so I held the door closed from the inside.

I believe you remained at the door of the cage and whispered continuously that this was not the life you had planned for me, until one day, by your grace, I let go of the door and stepped outside and into the refuge of your love. I will never look back!

"Pull me out of the net which they have secretly laid for me, For You are my strength" (Psalm 31:4).

I am praising your devotion and for the wonderous conversion you have initiated in my once-stolen life. As I have undergone, through your spirit, the necessary soul surgeries to remove the anxiety and fear-produced damage, you have met and exceeded my every hope for the love I needed to flourish. You have loved and supported me in ways that have brought about the most powerful responses from my heart. You have replaced the pain of abuse with the ability to forgive and to move forward without reservation into a new life filled with the security and encouragement I had been denied.

Thank you, Father, for reaching into my life and creating a longing I could not deny and for filling my soul with a thirst for closeness and understanding of whom my Creator is and why he has chosen me. You have expanded my life with purpose and new horizons that together we will explore. Teach me to imprint onto others the immense love that waits for them in the life-changing arms of God!

"It is God who arms me with strength, And makes my way perfect" (Psalm 18:32).

*W*atching thriving followers embrace relationships with you and others left me feeling like I was outside of the "church family" circle. I wanted to thrive, yet I lacked the means to accomplish new growth and sustaining fellowship.

You promised me during prayer one day that if I pressed in, you would build me a new life. Soon after, you began the pruning process, which left me feeling naked and exposed. I felt as if you had pruned my branches until they were nearly gone before you slowly and, with holy timing, began to graft in new growth.

Through the power of your spirit, I have learned to trust in your love for me and to realize a foundational truth. I can see clearly that when I had looked to the world as my source of hope, I began to very slowly, publicly, and painfully die on the vine. You have given me the hope and nurturing that comes through the sanctifying work of repenting, rescuing, healing, and repeating!

How blessed am I to walk through life and on to eternity with the all-loving God who has promised to never leave me. I will follow you in trust because I know you always have my very best in mind as you lead me!

"But I am like a green olive tree in the house of God; I trust in the mercy of God forever and ever" (Psalm 52:8).

*M*y foes, only painful reminders of my life, were evident before your intervention. You began the work of moving me through the lies and on to new-to-me truths, restoring the work the enemy had cleverly disguised by using intrusive and distorted thinking to keep me afraid, faithless, and stuck securely in the fear-based prison of my past.

You rescued me from my enemies, and you rescued me from myself! And in doing so, Father, you opened up a completely new life for me with the freedom to honestly embrace your love.

"He delivered me from my strong enemy, from those who hated me, for they were too strong for me" (Psalm 18:17).

I rushed, as if driven by winds of determination, willingly. I sought refuge with the wicked, whose mouths spoke of convincing devotion while their actions exploited the sanctity of my mind and body.

Father, where others profited through their evil deeds, you have breathed new life into those once-gaping wounds and created in me a source of fertile soil, where seeds of encouragement can be cultivated to help lift those who have fallen victim to wrongdoing.

You have rescued me from the pit of deception and purposely replaced my wounds with a heart filled with passion for the truth that you are the only source of true healing and hope for a new beginning.

"And the LORD shall help them and deliver them;
He shall deliver them from the wicked, And save
them, Because they trust in Him" (Psalm 37:40).

*I*t has truly been redemptive to crawl on the path the Lord faithfully provided, out from under the layers of sin and shame and straight into his waiting arms. Father, I remember a period during my recovery that I felt more secure in the known of the abuse than I did moving on to the unknown domain of your nature, where I truly believed there was no place for me.

You have shown me the greatest compassion I have ever known through your tender spirit, as you have loved me without condition. My meager hopes of your character were quickly surpassed by your steadfast reassurance that my history does not define me. I am defined by yours!

————

"The LORD is gracious and full of compassion,
Slow to anger and great in mercy" (Psalm 145:8).

My frequent and preferred path seemed to lead me in the opposite direction of the perfect plan you had designed for me. I sought peace and a life filled with happiness and contentment. By worldly standards, I found those things, but the worth of my portion was determined not by you, but by others who offered no better than they had consumed, a portion laced with a slow-acting poison that over time made my soul ill.

Father, it was hard for me to know how sick I had become until you helped me to see that my life was producing the same diseased fruit I had eaten, all the while thinking I was a guest at a fine banquet. Thank you, Lord, for never giving up on me and for teaching me to compare my portions to your righteous standard.

"Teach me to do Your will, For You are my God; Your Spirit is good. Lead me in the land of uprightness" (Psalm 143:10).

The persistent and unchanging love behind your faithfulness has been the lasting power that has restored my breath and calmed my heart whenever anxiety has tried to extinguish your peace from within me. A lifetime of depending on my own ability to articulate the ways of the world had left me riddled with doubt and reservations regarding my eternal value and the created purpose for my life.

Through the glory in your complete righteousness, I have learned that in my instability, I am made stable through your holiness. I am praising you, Father, for caring for me enough to let me fail and loving me enough to create in me a restored life.

"Yes, they shall sing of the ways of the Lord, For great is the glory of the Lord" (Psalm 138:5).

$\mathcal{M}$y heavenly blessing has been a nature that searches restlessly and a heart that pines for a relationship that is found in the silent moments. With closed eyes and emotions filled with expectancy, the world is quietly deferred.

I find myself in the serenity of your transforming love as I settle in on the holy ground at your feet. Resting in your presence and in those moments, I know instinctively that the stillness has connected my spirit with the Star Maker, the One who has lifted me to the lofty places where peace and healing are created and hope and faith thrive.

———————

"Seek the LORD and His strength; Seek His face evermore!" (Psalm 105:4).

As I was feeling like you measured only my mistakes, many years went by without a prayer. I was afraid to speak to you, believing a wrong word could be my last spoken, so I remained silent.

I found many ways to temporarily soothe the ache and loneliness in my heart; they didn't lead to fulfillment or connectedness, only more despair.

As my sin piled up, so did my anxiety and fear. They became the foundation upon which I built my life. I soon discovered that unless a house is built on the solid foundation of your Word, it will not stand up against a summer storm, much less the fury of winter.

As my anxiety raged out of control, my walls began to topple. One by one, they fell until there was nowhere for me to hide. You saw me at my worst and heard my desperate cries into the heavens, and without hesitation, you became my shelter. Your spirit came to dwell within me, and the rebuilding began. The foundation of truth was laid, and one by one, the walls of the temple went up. Father, you did so much more than hear my prayer. You saved my life!

"I have called upon You, for You will hear me, O God; Incline Your ear to me, and hear my speech" (Psalm 17:6).

The refuge I have found in your love has led me straight to the wonder of my blessed salvation. You have seen me through the greatest joys and the worst imaginable ordeals.

In the terror of darkest hours, you are faithful to remind me that I am not alone and that you are my source. You have restored my wounds to wholeness and cleansed my heart of the bitterness left behind from another life.

"But I am poor and needy; Yet the LORD thinks upon me. You are my help and my deliverer; Do not delay, O my God" (Psalm 40:17).

ather, as I sift through my feelings regarding your sovereign virtues, I struggle for understanding the righteous dignity of your character. I feel in gaining insight into the majesty of who you are, my best effort is the confusion one sees when looking at the backside of a tapestry. You are always so much more than my greatest expectation.

I am humbled and grateful that my power to enter into a relationship with you is not based on my capacities but yours. I have and am still learning to blindly trust you, not just when I am afraid and need my Father to rescue me, but in all areas of my life. Thank you for faithfully listening for the sound of my voice and for always making sure there is space under your wing for me.

"Hear me when I call, O God of my righteousness!
You have relieved me in my distress; Have mercy
on me, and hear my prayer" (Psalm 4:1).

I long to bow before your throne, to look into the face of the One whom I have envisioned in my mind, displaying love and kindness in a million different ways. You are holy and without rival of another who is worthy of the name Savior. There is nothing that compares to the atmosphere that accompanies your presence. It is tender and peaceful yet powerful!

With you for me, I know I can accomplish for your glory all that you desire. By your example, I have seen grace and mercy in action as it has unfolded and become manifest in my own testimony. Were it not for you, Father, I would have healed broken, forever stuck in the bondage of emotional pain. I want to share with others the mercy I have found through your love!

"But as for me, I will come into Your house in the multitude of Your mercy; In fear of You I will worship toward Your holy temple" (Psalm 5:7).

The Creator of the Universe delights in me? To even think this would have once felt as if it were as foreign a concept as milking a butterfly.

As staggering as this was to believe, it is nonetheless true. You do delight in me! Your love is the very essence of who you are, and through that love, I have become the heir to the vast riches of your grace, mercy, and forgiveness.

I have been blessed with your provision in ways that I have only ever heard about, the kind of provision that first required your death in order to allow this gift to be offered.

Thank you, Jesus, for providing me with all you had to offer, your love through your life. Help me do for others as you have done for me, to give all I am called to give.

————————

"He also brought me out into a broad place; He delivered me because He delighted in me" (Psalm 18:19).

*M*ore numerous than the stars are the profound love of their Inventor. You are the biographer of my life, the One who cast my character into motion inside of my mother's womb.

As I seek your embrace in the stillness of the night, I am comforted by the promise that you are bigger than anything forged against me. This is reflected in the sheer radiance and number of the stars, which fill the night's sky.

Anxiety is my worthy opponent! As I weep from the fear of the enclosing battle, I feel my air begin to fade as my heart races. With my last breath, it is you, the Master Host, that I call, and I breathe in your love, restoring me to the peace that is mine. Because of the cross, I stand with you in favor and honor as the enemy retreats.

"By the word of the Lord the heavens were made, And all the host of them by the breath of His mouth" (Psalm 33:6).

*Y*ou have delivered me from abuse, trauma, and isolation. Yet none of these compare to the moment you rescued me from the bitter poverty that filled my soul. In my isolation, I cried out in desperation, and you awoke within me eyes that could see and ears that could hear the sounds of rebirth as you breathed new life into my exhausted body.

I will forever be grateful, as I now thrive in the new life you once promised me has filled with a harvest of potential. Help me to be mindful as I bask in my blessings, to never get so comfortable that my gratitude is replaced with a sense of entitlement.

Help me, Father, to have an attitude of heart-rendering obedience and the spirit-led courage to embrace your will in my life as I encounter those who are also struggling to see and hear the love of God in their lives.

"But I am poor and needy; Make haste to me, O God! You are my help and my deliverer; O LORD, do not delay" (Psalm 70:5).

I remember a time when I felt sure that your love for me had faded, reduced to disapproval and judgment at the thought of me. The fear of your wrath and my inability to earn your love arrested any desire to put my trust into new relationships. My self-image mirrored my perceived assessment of the world around me, and this stronghold was my undoing.

Facedown at the base of the pit in which I had taken residence, I found you waiting for me. You had gone before me and waited for my free fall to end. You gave me new hope as you peeled back the layers of lies, exposing new truths, the greatest being. As I continued to envision your love through the perceptions that existed only in my mind, I maintained views of your love that limited my ability to love you, myself, or others unconditionally. Your divine love and patience have restored my life and given me purpose and hope.

"The LORD is merciful and gracious, Slow to anger, and abounding in mercy" (Psalm 103:8).

So many times, I felt abandoned by you, and persuaded by condemnation, I was assured my prayers echoed into the abyss of space uninhabited by any love for me.

How could my perception be so far from the truth? I have for years believed the concerto of lies that played daily performances in my mind.

Your unconditional love was never far. It was always hidden just on the other side of the lies I had come to believe. Your love is no longer held back by a dam of deception. It flows through me, healing wounds and nourishing my desire to share the message of the everlasting hope I have found in you.

"The LORD will perfect that which concerns me; Your mercy, O LORD, endures forever; Do not forsake the works of Your hands" (Psalm 138:8).

*T*hank you, Father, for the grace that made it possible for me to see the importance of living life within your blessing. You are my refuge; it is your lap that I run to when fear overtakes me. Your welcome embrace is the air that fills my lungs and the sparkle that others see.

I have tried to live life with a divided heart, securing my eternal passage while enjoying the enticements of my flesh. Because of your grace, I am free, and because of the hope that dwells within me, I am able to see that the world only leaves a slow and painful death to the recipient whose name you do not know. Exalted far above all of creation is the God whose promised hope is my inheritance.

"That I may see the benefit of Your chosen ones, That I may rejoice in the gladness of Your nation, That I may glory with Your inheritance" (Psalm 106:5).

Father, cleanse my soul so I would be mindful of trespassing against the covenant of your sovereign Word. Help me to honor the greatest commandment and let my heart be filled with uncontaminated love as I grasp at the root of the bitterness that thrives in my heart.

Forgive me for embracing the wrong done to me. Help me to lay those memories at your feet as you release me from the strongholds of my past and fill me with new light and a hope to share of a love that will forever extinguish the fiery arrows shot from the bow of desolation.

———

"Oh, let the wickedness of the wicked come to an end, But establish the just; For the righteous God tests the hearts and minds" (Psalm 7:9).

I have said in both word and deed, "You are my God," to so many things throughout my life. The gods I worshiped have always been a stark reflection of my true nature and the unjustified labels I assigned to you.

It took many years for me to understand that I lacked both a repentant heart and the life-changing understanding of who you are and what you have sacrificed for me. The ransom you paid for my sin was great. I realize that your love is far beyond my understanding, yet I believe that you would have paid the ransom of your only Son even if it were I alone that stood to be redeemed.

Thank you, Abba Father, for shining your light of truth on the gods in my life and for helping me to remove them from the throne of my heart. You alone reign!

———————

"But as for me, I trust in You, O LORD; I say, 'You are my God'" (Psalm 31:14).

*L*ord, you helped me to understand that my fortress built from fear was only as strong as the doubts that bound the insecurities to my soul and ultimately pushed out faith and hope.

I have suffered the agony of shaming isolation rather than acknowledge that the fear that had encircled me was not a fortress but a prison cell. The masquerade of empty laughter and joy substituted for the heartfelt praise of knowing that the God who created me was waiting to meet me right where I was.

Thank you, Father, for healing my soul and restoring my mind so I can now see your glory as it manifests itself all around me. I pray that others would go to the door of their prison cell and knock!

———

"The LORD of hosts is with us; The God of Jacob is our refuge. Selah" (Psalm 46:11).

I am praising your holy name at this moment as I reflect on the countless years I have spent wandering in the wilderness apart from the peace that comes from an obedient and surrendered walk in your presence.

Thank you, Lord, for the patient guidance of the Spirit as he led me out of the turmoil of a shattered life in the valley of hopelessness and back onto the narrow path, which your love and guidance light.

Faithfully you have led me daily into a deeper contentment and greater understanding of my need for a love relationship with Abba Father.

"For this is God, Our God forever and ever; He will be our guide Even to death" (Psalm 48:14).

The outward battles that created inward storms tore apart my belief in a God who died for me. As my mind waged war in the depth of my soul, fear and anxiety ruled where faith should have. Certain you embraced all prayers but mine, I felt abandoned by the One who held my only chance for deliverance.

Father, you have brought me through the worst possible misery, which I endured alone in my belief that you had turned your back on me, and even worse that my suffering was in part a result of your wrath.

Forgive me, Lord, for receiving the lie that you are capable of punishing those who are beaten down by life. I stand today not from the lies I believed but because of your love and grace.

"You, who have shown me great and severe troubles, Shall revive me again, And bring me up again from the depths of the earth" (Psalm 71:20).

I am so grateful for a Father's love as the world delivers blow after hope-shattering blow. Your promises are the only solid rock upon which I can anchor my faith to. When my heart is anxious and heavy, your love grounds me to the knowledge that your ways are beyond my simple understanding.

I trust in that love, even when I believe with all confidence that my heart hears what the spirit did not say. While the outcomes are so very different, I rest in the peace that when you override the desires of my heart, it is for reasons that you alone know are for my best. I take comfort in knowing that my heavenly Father is with me always.

"Our fathers trusted in You; They trusted, and You delivered them" (Psalm 22:4).

As my conception of maturity began to deviate from how my life was actually unfolding, I felt like diseased fruit that draped hopelessly on the vine amidst a beautifully developed crop that was ready for harvest.

Thank you, Father, for your careful observance of my circumstances. You knew how and when to work out the details of healing my wounds, through the loving care of your spirit and the followers you placed in my life. I am so grateful for the value you have seen in me when I have seen none. Help me to be aware of those who drape hopelessly on the vine, in need of your healing touch.

"What is man that You are mindful of him, And the son of man that You visit him?" (Psalm 8:4).

The one-of-a-kind nature that you knit into my soul was long ago altered from that which you had intended. Carrying damages known only to you, my heart yearned for the love and acceptance that proved again and again to be a familiar version of my past. Through the lens of abuse and rejection, I sought out the known rather than the unknown love of my heavenly Father.

Decades of surviving on emotional scraps, while seeking to repurpose the scars left from the toxic involvement with the darkest form of deviance, left me feeling like a house without a foundation as I anchored myself to resentment, believing I was unacceptable to God or surely he would have rescued me.

After years of checking off the prayer box and the church attendance box, I realized you do not live in those boxes, but in every crack I fell through. Every time I felt abandoned in life, you were there. You were not the representative of the men I had come to fear. You were the standard that had been cast aside in pursuit of selfish ambitions, just as I had been.

Thank you, Father, for designing me with the strength to survive and the desire to obey.

"In the day when I cried out, You answered me,
And made me bold with strength in my soul"
(Psalm 138:3).

*Y*our love is a beacon, casting the light of hope to a lost world. No matter how far from you I have strayed, your light shining through others has always been a tangible marker pointing me home.

As your grace and mercy continue to daily wash away the world in me, I am filled with thanksgiving for the gift I have been given. I didn't earn it; nor did I deserve it. Yet eternal love flowed freely from your heart, and through the cross, you declared that I am yours for all eternity. Through your love, Father, you pursued me and continually provide safety and shelter as you renew my mind after your own character.

Help me, Father, to walk in the fullness of your love, and as I serve you, I will sing praises to your name, giving you glory in all things.

"Oh, give thanks to the God of heaven! For His mercy endures forever" (Psalm 136:26).

elp me to keep my eyes focused as you guide me through this turning point with expectancy while you outline the details of this unfolding life lived in crisis. Recognizing your presence, whether silent or thunderous, as the unrivaled King of Kings, is the rock in which daily I build my new house.

With sword drawn or in the shelter of your wing, equip me to view trials with expectancy as I wait for triumphs. Fill me with the peace that comes from knowing that my God reigns and that I am precious in his sight. The day will come when every knee is bent as the world acknowledges the existence of and declares King Jesus is Lord God Almighty.

"For He shall give His angels charge over you, To keep you in all your ways" (Psalm 91:11).

*W*alking in the splendor of youth, while seeking adoration and acceptance, seemed at the time to nourish most, if not all, of my vital taste buds for a life well-lived. The yardstick for this diet of self-love ran out about the same time I began to see mortality cresting on the horizon.

The awareness of how temporal a moment spent in idol worship is compared to an eternity living under the righteousness of a just God seems to bring life into focus. Father, help me to worship only you and to receive nourishment not from the world but from quiet time spent in your Word that I could in all truth proclaim the good news of your sacrificial love to those who have yet to receive you.

———————

"O LORD, our Lord, How excellent is Your name in all the earth, Who have set Your glory above the heavens!" (Psalm 8:1).

The choices made in an instant sometimes have the greatest impact on our witness and those around us whom God was intending to touch in one way or another. A word of encouragement, an act of kindness, and the overlooked opportunities God provides to shape our spiritual character while blessing others should be viewed as holy opportunities.

For me, it often boils down to a faith issue, lacking enough trust to put myself in positions that generate anxiety. Faith is all about courage and trusting in the love of our Creator!

Today, I chose fear over faith and wound up losing the blessing of watching God work in my life. That alone would have been hard, but add to it that I essentially threw God and His promises under the proverbial bus. I chose instead to manipulate the circumstance for my own comfort, with the illusion-based hope of returning to a place of peace.

God knew this was going to happen! I sure didn't! The sequence of fear, decision, consequence, shame, repentance, and tears came full circle so fast that I couldn't believe how quickly my heart brought me to my knees. If I had just stayed on course, God had my best outcome planned. I just needed to trust and receive.

Thank you, Father, for the convictions and consequences in life. Even your discipline is sweet. I pray for faith that chases out all fear. Help me to stare down the barrel of life and claim your promises as the truth that sets me free.

———

"The LORD looks from heaven; He sees all the sons of men" (Psalm 33:13).

The declarations of the Lord are more profound than the raging sea to a heart that is fertile and postured to discern the sacred sound of his voice.

So many times, I sailed into the eye of the storm, confident in my own ability to navigate the waters ahead. Yet in my pride, unable to see that I could not even comprehend the dark current that separated me from you, naturally these obstacles swept me off course and into stormy waters.

As I was building my testimony, you helped me to see the storms as an opportunity for sanctification. With a repentant heart, I pressed in, allowing your presence to fill and restore my soul as I found rest in the shelter of your love and protection.

"He calms the storm, So that its waves are still" (*Psalm 107:29*).

he everlasting love that flows from the story of mercy and hope, which began in Bethlehem and is made possible through the empty tomb, continues to grow in my heart. You faithfully rolled the stone away, which kept me in darkness, to the truth of my created purpose. My life was gradually slipping by, as the world, with my permission, defined my value by ever-shifting standards, set far below the price that was paid for me.

The refuge you have provided is secure and unchanged by the regression in the world. Your love is the same yesterday, today, and always. Your perfect love casts out all fear!

"Oh, how great is Your goodness, Which You have laid up for those who fear You, Which You have prepared for those who trust in You In the presence of the sons of men!" (Psalm 31:19).

*Y*ou are the stream of living water, providing life and giving nourishment to my body. As I listen for the sound of your voice, I am reminded that the power of your Sovereign Deity flows through me with the quiet disposition and patience of the Master Architect, dividing light and darkness.

Mold me, Lord, using your character as a template so I would see in others that which you see and with a sense of urgency to be the vessel you use to give sight to the blind. You are the Potter, and I surrender myself to the life-restoring wheel of your love.

"Truly my soul silently waits for God; From Him comes my salvation" (Psalm 62:1).

ather, help me to weep from a heart of forgiveness and grace. You have been faithful to restore the poverty in my soul by healing and providing the hunger that can only be satisfied through a relationship with you. Shine your living light on my path and fill me with holy energy as I pursue the calling you have placed in my heart.

I weep now in gratitude that you have loved me with an all-healing love, a love that embraced me even before you began knitting me together in my mother's womb.

Let grace for those who have wounded me in their brokenness abound from the place in my heart, which was once filled with resentment, and fill me with a yearning to see them restored and walking in the light of your love.

———

"Depart from me, all you workers of iniquity;
For the LORD has heard the voice of my weeping"
(Psalm 6:8).

A fortress built from a life of fear dwells in the vacuum of a persistent storm. I have sought refuge from the gale of the storm within the emptiness of my man-made lodging. Alone with my fear and insecurities, I had fallen victim to the enemy's destructive plan to rob, kill, and destroy.

Your all-embracing love has exposed the deception of the adversary. A refuge designed by man is perishable, lacking in fortitude, while that which is designed and built by God will stand forever.

Thank you, Father, for faithfully exposing the lies of the enemy and establishing your holy residence within my heart. You are my eternal fortress; alone in You do I have absolute trust.

"I will say of the LORD, 'He is my refuge and my fortress; My God, in Him I will trust'" (Psalm 91:2).

When I am poor in spirit, you who are rich in love are faithful to restore me from the affluence of your boundless grace. Just as my cry for help feels incessant, so has your love persistently met me at the core of my need. You have taken my fears and replaced them with the healing truth of who I am in You.

I am safe! I am loved! And I am eternally with Jesus, seated at the right hand of the throne of almighty God, created by him, for him, from his perfect design and longing for family.

Lord, fill me with the blind obedience to follow the sound of your voice, trusting as you guide me to those who are poor in spirit and seeking, like myself, the richness of your love.

"This poor man cried out, and the LORD heard him, And saved him out of all his troubles" (Psalm 34:6).

My shelter was warm and dry, but it was not a refuge, and the shield I bore was one created from a legacy of suffering. The heaviness of my shield led me toward a life surrounded by self-soothing idols and for many years far away from fellowship with my heavenly Father.

You saw through the convincing veneer of contentment. Through your love, I have been reunited with my Creator, and under your wing, I have found my armor forged through love.

Thank you, Father, for extinguishing the power the evil one held over my heart. By shining the light of truth into the darkness, you were faithful to cast out the enemy as you took your rightful place on the throne of my heart.

———

> *"But You have seen, for You observe trouble and grief, To repay it by Your hand. The helpless commits himself to You; You are the helper of the fatherless"* (Psalm 10:14).

*H*iding from any opportunity for betrayal to tiptoe into my heart, I safely tucked myself away from life and relationship. I sat quietly, hoping to be found by the entity that would make my life complete.

Being loved and secure and wanting for nothing was my heart's desire. As I watched life passing by from the security of my hiding place, I realized I wasn't hidden at all. My heart, my soul, and my location were in plain view of my Creator.

As I was watching life and all the perceived danger, he was watching me and seizing opportunities to restore the dry and barren soil of my soul with the rich and fertile ground in which he would begin planting seeds of change that would one day produce a harvest in my life.

Patiently waiting, he began tilling out my fear and replacing it with faith. As he continued to till out the weeds, making the soil in my heart tender and warm, I realized the love and security I was looking for was with me all along. Father, you are the Way and the Truth and the desire of my heart!

"Deliver me, O LORD, from my enemies; In You I take shelter" (Psalm 143:9).

*I*n moments of tribulation, holiness can seem obscured by darkness, making it impossible to feel the presence of God. For me, when the glory of his deeds rises above my faith, all hope for peace is gone, leaving me with a diminished capacity to receive new truths.

For literally decades I suffered not at the hand of the enemy, but the wrong thinking, which permeated my mind from the wounds in my soul. I was aware that there was a hollowness inside and that my life at times was, at best, just limping along. Yet the courage to offer the Lord a surrendered heart required more trust than I could allow.

Over time, the majesty of your jealous love has filled my soul, and the once-inability to trust you has been replaced with a righteous hunger, a thirst for your presence, and a timeless peace.

"His work is honorable and glorious, And His righteousness endures forever" (Psalm 111:3).

*E*ncourage my heart and lift my thoughts to a place of other thinking and let my words reflect your love and not the residue of my own circumstances. Lord, just as you are the light of the world, help me also to be a light and source of encouragement to those near me. Direct my path to those in need of the eternal promise that they would find their source of everlasting peace in your love.

Like the sunrise chasing away the darkness, I pray that your love would have a ripple effect as it makes its way through the lives of those in need of your peace.

"The LORD will give strength to His people; The LORD will bless His people with peace" (Psalm 29:11).

I am reflecting on God's goodness and how faithful he has been to restore that which the enemy meant to destroy. I am a new creation! Time heals all wounds? No! Jesus's love and only his love can restore the deep wounds left by others.

Redeem my heart, Lord, that I would see creation through your eyes when I see the darkest parts of humanity. Help me, Lord, to walk in the light of your truth that if it weren't for the darkest parts of humankind, the cross would not have been needed. The world is crying out in despair for the hope that can only be found in you.

I pray that you would help me to see Pentecost with a fresh revelation and to invite your spirit in to continue the work of restoration and redemption, making it possible for me to be a witness of your profound power and love.

———

"O Israel, hope in the LORD; For with the LORD there is mercy, And with Him is abundant redemption" (*Psalm 130:7*).

The wellspring of your affection never runs dry; it flows freely over me and through me as much or as little as my heart is willing to receive your endless love.

How many times have I taken your mercy for granted? Not today, Lord! Seeking instead the luxury of my free will only to find out, as Eve did, that the smallest choices can lead to disaster.

Help me, Lord, to above all seek first your kingdom and to walk in joyful obedience toward the field, to work with you to bring in the harvest.

———

"The LORD is good to all, And His tender mercies are over all His works" (Psalm 145:9).

*Y*ou have delivered me again and again as I sought fulfillment for my soul. Each gesture of eternal love has produced a harvest of hope and purpose in my life.

Longing to reap the richness of your presence, I am reminded of times I would circumvent my highest good by viewing your sovereignty through the narrow limitations of my own thoughts.

I am grateful for the spirit's redemptive work of peeling back layer after layer of the past until finally the darkness that once eclipsed my mind and hid the truth is overcome with perfect light, revealing what the enemy could not hide, the intensity of God's love.

"In You, O Lord, I put my trust; Let me never be ashamed; Deliver me in Your righteousness" (Psalm 31:1).

Frequently I have found myself on the precipice, looking within and hoping to find the security of my next step, only to rediscover that my shortsighted best efforts had once again left a huge division between God's perfect will and my meager and often self-sabotaging attempts to find fulfillment.

Show me, Lord, how to put aside my own ambitions and to joyfully surrender to your perfect plan by removing the self-importance from my heart and the need to be gratified in a world that prides itself on many gods when the sacrificial love of King Jesus is needed.

———

"Preserve my life, for I am holy; You are my God; Save Your servant who trusts in You!" (Psalm 86:2).

*I*t is difficult to fathom unconditional love when the watermark in that reservoir has remained at a low point for a lifetime. The Lord, because of his love, has been faithful beyond understanding. He has raised the water table in my soul to new heights and, with it, a deep appreciation for his generous nature.

He is worthy of trust, and never has he failed to work all things for my best. He has abundantly provided for me and walked through each valley, restoring my soul and turning my once-fearful heart toward him.

"Return to your rest, O my soul, For the LORD has dealt bountifully with you" (Psalm 116:7).

*M*y soul, wounded in battle long ago, remained crippled through the injuries inflicted by others, leaving me afraid to trust God with my heart and specifically my life. I held him responsible for the harm that had been done.

In his wisdom, he saw the pains of my past and the longing in my heart for the truth and acceptance that I searched for unsuccessfully. In his righteousness, he pursued me, and through his love, he changed me by teaching me to confront the lies of the past with the truth of his faithful Word. The fraud of the enemy cannot hold the ground that God claims as his!

———

"He restores my soul; He leads me in the paths of righteousness For His name's sake" (Psalm 23:3).

You met me where I was, and the sobering truth of your love over time penetrated the lies that were creating my instability. At every turn, it seemed I came face-to-face with the intervention of the Holy Spirit as he convicted me. This confused and scared me, for his promptings felt substantial, mistaking them with the condemnation I had known my entire life.

He was faithful to teach me that while conviction stems from love and leads to repentance, condemnation is from the devil and leads to despair and resentment. This conflict was real, and it took some time before the enemy lost his destructive grip.

At first, I wanted to continue to live the lies because they were familiar, but more than that, I wanted peace. Through your love, my life was elevated from that dark place to my new home, seated next to my King Jesus.

"Among the gods there is none like You, O Lord; Nor are there any works like Your works" (Psalm 86:8).

He has conquered death, and with his body, he has paid the ransom for my life. The cruelty of long ago, now drenched with Christ's blood, can no longer reach me. With each holy embrace, the space in my soul where fear once thrived, only the scars are left behind as a reminder to identify that pain as I see it in others and to offer the Source of hope I have found.

The enemy no longer has the power to torment me in the night or shame me into isolation by day. I now celebrate the stronghold I have joyfully surrendered to Jesus. I have traded the chains of bondage and, with it, the hopelessness of a life without purpose for the honor of serving my Redeemer who has delivered me from harm.

———

> "My lovingkindness and my fortress, My high tower and my deliverer; My shield and the One in whom I take refuge, Who subdues my people under me" (Psalm 144:2).

I am reminded of the hymn "When the Saints Go Marching In" and hold firm to the truth that every step I take is made possible by the prevailing power of the Lord.

Praise be to God for his mercies never end and his love for me is based on his nature and not my character. I am blessed beyond measure that my Creator's desire to love me and to remain true to his promises were never contingent on my love for him.

I have failed in both word and deed and have been forgiven and restored out of the abundance of his grace. Today I walk redeemed, as the saints before me, looking to do the work of the Master.

———

"Cast your burden on the LORD, And He shall sustain you; He shall never permit the righteous to be moved" (Psalm 55:22).

Spending a life wedged between fear and the certainty that my Creator saw me through the same lens as I saw myself, I was angry in my belief that he only heard the sin, not the sinner's cry for love.

Each acknowledgment of my misdeed led me that much closer to his wrath. See me, hear me, and restore me, God! Show me that you died for me too.

Your tender love once confused me. I sought to understand the perfection of your grace while fully embracing my own version of obscurity. No longer do I carry the scars of conditional love. You have penetrated the darkness of that lie with the light of truth.

You have helped me exchange the fear of your wrath for the foundational truth that I have been adopted into the family of God and that my greatest credit is that I belong to you, Father.

---

*"Because He has inclined His ear to me, Therefore
I will call upon Him as long as I live" (Psalm 116:2).*

*Y*ou have ushered me through the layers of the past and moved me to a sure foundation through the cross. I walk as a new creation in the image of my Lord.

Fear and anxiety once held me hostage, surviving daily on the hopes of my own limited resources. I now sit with Jesus at the right hand of God Almighty, rejoicing in his love.

While I am not a stranger to fear, it no longer holds the power to rock my faith, steering me away from the goodness of my heavenly Father. He is faithful to meet all my needs! He has restored my soul! Show me, Father, what can I do for the kingdom today.

"Blessed is the man whose strength is in You,
Whose heart is set on pilgrimage" (Psalm 84:5).

The same hands outstretched on the cross for my sins are now securely holding me so that when I stumble, I don't fall. Once my life felt like the descent would not come to an end. In my foolishness, I believed a relationship with the Lord would lack the rewarding life, filled with the freedoms I sought in the world.

The devious plots of the enemy and wrong thinking led me down the path of destruction. It is only through God's grace and mercy that I walk in the new life he has created for me. It is with a contented heart that I seek to bring light and love into the world through his guidance and the spirit-filled passions within me.

"Let Your hand become my help, For I have chosen Your precepts" (Psalm 119:173).

There is no way to outrun the spirit of the living God; there is no hiding place that is not visible or truth of the heart that is not felt by God through our worship.

Years spent running only helped me to see that it was my flesh that I was running from. The pain, the shame, and the guilt were more than enough to derail my shallow faith. Being caught between the fear of hell and the torment that was my daily companion left me buried under condemnation.

In looking back, my heart is overwhelmed with gratitude for the intercessory prayers that went up on my behalf. Thank you, Father, for hearing from others what I could not say and for helping me to find my way home.

———

"Where can I go from Your Spirit? Or where can I flee from Your presence?" (Psalm 139:7).

imes too numerous to count, I found myself in the fear-created domicile of my mind, struggling to find even the smallest shred of hope. In my disillusionment, I called out to you, Lord, to fill me with your peace as I waited, with expectation fading for my breakthrough.

What my faith lacked, my fear consumed. As I searched through the scriptures for life-giving hope, I cried, "Speak to me, Lord. Lift this load from me, for it is beyond my capacity to carry this darkness one more step. Please hurry, and let me rejoice as you fill my soul with the joy of your presence."

Thank you for again showing your faithful love and awakening my mind to the truth that my body is your sanctuary and my place in your dwelling was established long ago and purchased with your precious blood.

"Lord, you have been our dwelling place throughout all generations" (Psalm 90:1).

For brief periods, my eyes were fixed on a variety of things, none worthy of eternal reward. Grateful that the fear that piloted my path was substantial, like the prodigal, I continued to return to the shelter of the Lord, for he is my sanctuary and my strength.

Father, the love you share is woven into the celestial fabric of who you are. It is the essence of your teachings and the pinnacle of the gospel truth.

Thank you, Lord, for greater are you who is in me than he who is in the world. You have spared me from death! Help me to guide others into the waiting arms of the one true God that they may also find life.

"But my eyes are upon You, O God the Lord; In You I take refuge; Do not leave my soul destitute" (Psalm 141:8).

*T*hrough you, I see all of creation with awesome wonder. You who constructed the universe also created the space in my soul, which remained empty until the moment I responded to your call.

The Lord God Almighty, ruler of heaven and earth, is a jealous God. He is the lover of my soul, the comforter that rushes in when the world rushes out. Father, you have been my faithful beacon in every storm. Use me to assure others that they are loved.

"My help comes from the LORD, Who made heaven and earth" (Psalm 121:2).

*Y*ou knew the inception of my insecurities and met me at that place by responding each time I called your name. You have been faithful to meet my needs, not based on my timing as I would have wanted, but timing perfectly aligned with what was best for my spiritual character and your holy plan. You have built me up in faith through your faithfulness and love through your acceptance.

I pray continually for the purification of my heart that my actions would echo the grace of my Father in heaven. I rejoice with boldness that your love has made all life possible!

---

*"Because Your lovingkindness is better than life,
My lips shall praise You" (Psalm 63:3).*

I am overcome once more by fear, as my mind recoils from toxic pockets. The fallen world has left more than one imprint on my soul. With a racing heart and sweating palms, I cry out to you, to end the battle of wills that exists inside my mind. Help me, Lord, to heed the words of the spirit and surrender completely to the foot of the cross, the fear, anxiety, and most of all my own dependence on seeking my will over yours.

You exchanged your life for mine. The cost to you was high, yet you offer it freely to me. Let me be a continual witness to the hope and healing that can only be found in the glory of the Lord, whose love shines through the hearts of those who succumb to the heavenly power of your still, small voice.

"There are many who say, 'Who will show us any good?' LORD, lift up the light of Your countenance upon us" (Psalm 4:6).

ou have never failed me! You are exalted above every circumstance whether contrived by the enemy or developed in the darkness of my heart. I lift up praises to you, Father, for faithfully nourishing me, as I work out the details of my own salvation.

You who makes all things new have replaced the wounds of my past with new life and a new faith-based purpose. I pray that the fruit of your spirit would be visible to others as I boldly seek to share of the grace I have been given by the invisible God who has sustained and created all things through the power of your boundless love.

"Who made heaven and earth, The sea, and all that is in them; Who keeps truth forever" (Psalm 146:6).

I will praise evermore as I roll up my sleeves and press into the race before me, gratefully receiving your promises of strength and courage. The unforeseen lies around every corner bring with them unexpected emotions and opportunities. I rest in knowing that you go before me.

Father, let my faith rise to each new challenge. Remove the strongholds the enemy has deceived me into believing are my burden to bear.

Holy Spirit, free me to soar with boldness alongside the holy army of saints and help me to endure as your love is my witness.

"He saved them from the hand of him who hated them, And redeemed them from the hand of the enemy" (Psalm 106:10).

I set myself adrift from your will, choosing instead to follow my heart, knowing you see in the light what I sought to hide in the darkness. My deeds transgressed against the honor you are due.

My head was low with shame until your words pierced my soul, and like a hallowed salve, your spirit within me calmed my inner fears and spoke truth over my actions.

My shame was mine alone, but the victory I have found in you is rejoiced throughout the heavens. Show me how to be an encouragement to those who, like me, have chosen other than your perfect will. Thank you, Father, for your vigilant love!

"He fashions their hearts individually; He considers all their works" (Psalm 33:15).

*L*ord, let not my fear of you overshadow the amazing love that led you to Calvary, yet let it be a guide to keep me from traveling off the narrow path. Father, prepare the soil in my heart. As we walk, make it rich and fertile so fellow travelers would know my God by my fruit.

———————

"Blessed is every one who fears the LORD, Who walks in His ways" (Psalm 128:1).

The victories have been my greatest challenge and my sweetest reward as they have brought me into your presence. Restoration and healing were all along in your plans, to shower me with the redemptive love of the cross.

Conditional love left me riddled with doubt, and abuse completed my brokenness with overflowing shame. You were there! Every moment I thought I was alone in my pain and rebellion, you were there! Gripped by perishing mortality, my soul longed for the reassurance of love. You were there! Protected by your blood and sealed with your holy symbol, you were there!

Through the darkest moments, as you peeled back the layers of this broken life. I sought my horizon just over the glory of the mountaintop, and I found you, my Shepherd, on the hill.

"As the mountains surround Jerusalem, So the Lord surrounds His people From this time forth and forever" (Psalm 125:2).

*Y*ou protect my mind from the fiery arrows that daily seek to destroy the sweet communion within the temple I share with your Spirit.

Inside this sanctuary, you give me shelter from every prevailing storm and a place to rest when there is none. I live and breathe the air that you alone provide. How grateful I am to have a Father who loves me as you do.

Guide my steps to those in need of a refuge that I might tell them that the perfect love, which casts out all fear is found in the embrace of the Most High.

---

*"You who fear the L*ORD*, trust in the L*ORD*; He is their help and their shield" (Psalm 115:11).*

With outstretched hands praising the glory of what it means to live a transformed life in relationship with the one true God, I walk in fullness, sharing God's love.

Lord, I place the stronghold of fear, which I have felt most of my life, at your feet and receive in its place the righteous fear that is my birthright in Christ. Let it be an everlasting gateway to insights.

Let all who hear your voice live each day with eager anticipation of what unique purpose and plans you have predestined in love.

———

"The fear of the LORD is the beginning of wisdom; A good understanding have all those who do His commandments. His praise endures forever" (Psalm 111:10).

*A*ll things pass away, yet your name lives on, echoing across the universe through the miracle of heavenly creation.

To the world, you are God. In the hearts of the saints, you are Abba Father, Savior, friend, Redeemer, and the defender of the weak and rescuer to the oppressed. From the garden to New Jerusalem, let your praises be sung and your name exalted.

———

"For the LORD is good; His mercy is everlasting, And His truth endures to all generations" (Psalm 100:5).

When you bring the joy of your sanctuary into my heart, I come into the meditative presence of your Spirit. I feel completely at peace as your presence washes away the world, renewing both my body and soul.

Your majesty is more than I can comprehend, yet it is my yearning to be sanctified into your likeness. Show me, Lord, how to share your splendor with those who have yet to hear the call of the Master.

"Honor and majesty are before Him; Strength and beauty are in His sanctuary" (Psalm 96:6).

I depend on your daily instruction so I might live in obedience to your will for my life. It is through your divine guidance that I dwell in peace and safety, living a life far from the pitfalls that once engulfed me.

You are my Savior, and your love for me has changed my life. Forever I will sing your praises and seek your direction. I have faith in your protection, and I trust that you always hold my best interest firmly in sight.

"I will instruct you and teach you in the way you should go; I will guide you with My eye" (Psalm 32:8).

You are my safe place, my eternal salvation, and my quiet refuge during the storms in life. I trust only in you, for daily you have proven over and over to be a faithful and loving Father. By staying steadfast and true to the course ahead, you have shown me the path to glory and have walked each step with me as I continue to seek wholeness. In you there is no fear; there is only peace.

When anxiety begins to cast a shadow over the joy of having your Holy Spirit within me, I call on your name, and instantly I begin to feel your peace move over me. How I love to feel the warmth of your spirit. Father, your loving embrace is tender beyond anything I could ever imagine. Daily Lord, you shower me with your love and blessings. As I hear your words, my heart responds with a joy-filled longing to be nearer to you. Lord, with a grateful heart I give thanks for your mercy.

_____

"The LORD is my light and my salvation—whom shall I fear? The LORD is the stronghold of my life—of whom shall I be afraid?" (Psalm 27:1).

*L*ord, give me right thinking and an obedient heart as I lay my life, fears, intrusive thoughts, and resentment all down at the altar in obedience and surrender to you and for you, as you did when you laid your life down at the cross for me.

Oh, that I would have passion to pursue the gifts of spirit and purpose as I follow your command so I may serve you with a richness that can only be explained through the declaration of your love as I learn to trust your voice.

———

"Offer the sacrifices of righteousness, And put your trust in the LORD" (Psalm 4:5).

*Y*ou have searched my heart and know my every thought; my heart rejoices that through the power of the name of Jesus, all fear and anxiety within me departs at the acknowldgment of your holy presence. Darkness cannot remain where the light of the world dwells! Help me to press in to the reward of fullness in your love as I lean in to submit myself into the care of my all-knowing Creator.

Thank you for your everlasting promise that you will never leave me or depart from me.

"Search me, O God, and know my heart; Try me, and know my anxieties" (Psalm 139:23).

Finding lasting fulfillment within my own personal and very limited emotional resources was something I found perpetually disheartening. When I finally came to the end of my search, I found myself exhausted but with the fresh realization that it was altogether not possible without God's all-consuming healing embrace to become a thriving and joy-filled holy receptacle brimming with the light from God's life-changing love.

Lord, the relevant reminders you put in your Word of how faithful you are to watch over your flock and provide for the needs of your children bring comfort to me when I feel the pain of isolation and the fear of death.

Thank you that your love never ceases and your grace is new every morning. Thank you, Father, for being a God of new beginnings.

"This is the day that the Lord has made; We will rejoice and be glad in it" (Psalm 118:24).

Thank you for watching over me through your daily provision and abundant measure of grace. You have shown me how precious I am to you. Your undying love has chased away my fears and has over time created in me a trust for the God of truth.

Through you, I have sprouted the confidence of a holy awareness of the peace, safety, and protection of my Father. My heart is full of gratitude for the long-awaited place to rest where any threat of fear or harm rests on your sovereign shoulders and not mine.

"When I am afraid, I will trust in you" (Psalm 56:3).

Until the mercy of your healing touch rested gently on my troubled heart, I wondered in the darkness in tremendous despair. Alone I suffered in my misery until you lifted me from my brokenness, and in you, I have become victorious. There is none more righteous than you, O Lord. Your shield protects me, and your love continually guides me along solid and fertile ground.

In you, Lord, there is so much to be grateful for. I am blessed because of the grace you have shown me. It has given me life and renewed my tormented soul. With a child's grateful heart, I thank you, Father, for your tender yet mighty devotion.

"You have also given me the shield of Your salvation; Your right hand has held me up, Your gentleness has made me great" (Psalm 18:35).

*Y*our thoughts are always on me, thinking only of my best. You are my Father, Redeemer, Counselor, and friend. Lord, you are my compass, and with my eyes on you, I am guaranteed never to lose my way. With you carefully watching over me, I cannot fail. Blessed be the name of the Lord God my Savior.

———————

"I will cry out to God Most High, To God who performs all things for me" (Psalm 57:2).

I rejected the teaching of my childhood; instead I pursued numerous gods and searched desperately for the love that only stole my trust. Robbed of my innocence and betrayed by my lust, I found only regret. The love and acceptance I had sought were not to be found in the gods I had worshipped.

My Father taught me that when hope dies, it gives birth to truth. Truth leads to restoration; true healing is the beginning of wisdom.

Thank you, Lord, for inhabiting my heart. Continue giving me new and fresh revelation to the deeper love that exists in the heart of God that I, through your grace, may encourage those looking to find happiness through idols that you are their source.

"For all the gods of the peoples are idols, But the Lord made the heavens" (Psalm 96:5).

I reverence your amazing love and how you use your healing power to touch the lives of those who are deeply distressed and living in isolation. Thank you, Father, that when anxiety comes and builds up walls, sealing me in the darkest prison, you bring light and peace to free me from the storm. Help me to meditate on you as my only source of hope.

———

"You rule the raging of the sea; When its waves rise, You still them" (Psalm 89:9).

At times, I am so consumed with fear and anxiety that I feel my death corresponds to the beating of my heart. My pride fails me, as self has been reduced to humility, which follows the utter hopelessness in my own abilities.

I give you thanks for saving me again and again as anxious thoughts overtake me. I know you are with me and will walk beside me through every storm, creating and renewing a strength that only comes from the love of Calvary.

You are my source of comfort; you support me in my despair and lift me up through encouraging thoughts and appreciation for all you have done and continue to do for me. I praise your name for turning my weakness into strength, which daily seems to build my trust in you. You are a lamp that sheds the light of truth on my fears. In you, I have found hope at last.

"Yea, though I walk through the valley of the shadow of death, I will fear no evil; For You are with me; Your rod and Your staff, they comfort me" (Psalm 23:4).

I am so grateful that when I am in trouble, you never let my cries go unanswered. In your wisdom, you intercede, always having my best interest as your top priority. You spread your peace across me, and it blankets and protects me in safety as I find rest until my strength is restored. Thank you, Father, for always saving me; your mercy and love are faithful to cut short my suffering.

———

"Then they cried out to the Lord in their trouble, And He saved them out of their distresses" (Psalm 107:19).

You are my almighty God, and in your shadow, I gladly take rest, for it is there that my security lies. In your shadow, I have found love. You have given me rest when death was close. Father, you have faithfully protected me all my life. You have washed away my pain, and in return, you have offered me a fruitful life if I would just put my trust in you. I have eaten your fruit with thanksgiving in my heart.

"He who dwells in the secret place of the Most High shall abide under the shadow of the Almighty" (Psalm 91:1).

*F*ather, day by day, through your constant care, I have learned to put my trust and hope in you. I lay my life before you because I have learned that with you for me, who or what can come against me?

Through my weakness, I gain strength and victory through my growing faith in you. Your healing touch and the infilling of your love and mercy truly bring about transformation in my life. Thank you for saving me from the pain and suffering of my tribulation. I am eternally grateful for your daily blessing of shelter from my fears and anxieties.

"Now I know that the LORD saves His anointed; He will answer him from His holy heaven With the saving strength of His right hand" (Psalm 20:6).

As I follow you, Lord, I pray that my walk would continue to be a transformation of my mind, body, and spirit. Father in heaven, with my eyes firmly on you, it is my heart's desire that daily I would grow to be more like you, that my actions would be a reflection of your essence.

With humility, I thank you for all you have done and continue to do to bless me.

"Then they are glad because they are quiet; So He guides them to their desired haven" (Psalm 107:30).

As I sit here in my cozy writing room, surrounded by the warmth of cherrywood, family photos, and the trinkets that normally bring instant warmth to my heart, I am overwhelmed with the deep sadness, which for me seems to emerge alongside feelings of grief.

There are so many losses—family, fellowship, and finances. Yet I am struggling to find how and where to fit in, which has been my quest. It is an expedition that has spanned a lifetime. The presence of loneliness is heavy with truth as I reflect over the years.

Thank you, Father, for being faithful to your promise to catch your child, as I free-fall into this familiar valley. Through the faithful teaching of your spirit, I have come to a place of expectancy. Just as I felt forewarned that this free fall was about to begin, I am equally confident that I am not without my Creator. You are my comfort in this dark place, just as you will deliver me through the valley where the reward of my breakthrough is waiting.

You have shown me over the years that the blessings in valleys are the source of our growth. They are the Potter's wheel and the refining fires in life, and we should never avoid them, just the opposite. We should take hold of your faithful hand and together run like the wind down that hill. Our victories are waiting!

"Blessed is that man who makes the LORD his trust, And does not respect the proud, nor such as turn aside to lies" (Psalm 40).

efore I was conceived, you knew me! You have watched over me all the days of my life, counting even the hairs on my head. You have searched me and know my every thought. It is my plea that you would cast out any wickedness in my heart that keeps my spirit from growing and encompassing all that is pleasing in your sight.

"O LORD, You have searched me and known me"
(Psalm 139:1).

Glory be unto you, my Savior. You have redeemed me and lifted my anxious soul from the darkness and despair of my fears. Without you, there is sure death. In you, I have found life everlasting.

Lord, I am lost without your shield, for I alone cannot withstand the arrows of my foe, but in you, I have found victory. Set my course ahead, Father, that I might have a light heart to joyfully do your good works all the days of my life.

————

"But You, O Lord, are a shield for me, My glory and the One who lifts up my head" (Psalm 3:3).

Remove the shifting sand from beneath my feet, dear Lord, and make my steps firm. I desire to walk beside you, O Lord. Wherever you direct me, I shall go.

I want to be your hands and bring glory to your name in all I do. It is my prayer to be your good and faithful servant and that my life would be a living testament to your peace and love.

———

"The steps of a good man are ordered by the LORD,
And He delights in his way" (Psalm 37:23).

ost of my life I have felt displaced, as if in another place and time I would not have felt lost and dying. Convinced you were unconcerned with my pain and were disconnected from my torment, I doubted that I had any worth to you at all!

Slowly you began to appear, at first in small ways, and then a life-changing transformation began to happen in my heart. Through your compassion, I realized that your love is the key that has set me free. No longer is my life saturated with the fragrance of reeking decomposition.

You have breathed new and fresh life into my soul, where shame and guilt once held the chains to my captivity. I was never forgotten; nor was I absent from your sight. I now rejoice as I am a new creation, a beloved offering to my Savior. There's no more darkness and no more tears, only the sweet fragrance of love.

"He sent His word and healed them, And delivered them from their destructions" (Psalm 107:20).

My heart rejoices at the thought of you, Lord. How thankful I am that your love surrounds me. I desire to please you, Father, with every thought, action, and deed. May they bring me closer to you. My heart desires to know you better and to love you more. In your precious name I pray.

"Oh, give thanks to the Lord, for He is good! For His mercy endures forever" (Psalm 107:1).

When I am afraid, it is the shelter of your wing that I seek. In your name only I am able to claim victory over anxiety, for nothing can stand against you.

In my darkest moment, you surround me, filling my thoughts with a peace that surpasses all human understanding. You are always faithful to silence my fears and fill me with thoughts of your mercy and grace as you give your child comfort and rest from the storm within.

"I sought the LORD, and He heard me, And delivered me from all my fears" (Psalm 34:4).

Through the power of your love, lives are transformed, and in your strength, we rise up out of the depth of the darkness that once engulfed our lives.

Father, you are the Redeemer of the living. As I turn my eyes toward you, my fears fade, and my heart is lifted. Your name holds all of the glory and righteousness imaginable.

"Your God has commanded your strength; Strengthen, O God, what You have done for us" (Psalm 68:28).

From your love, the ultimate sacrifice was given so I could dwell with you eternally. I pray, Lord, that the work you do in me shall bring glory and honor to your name every day of my life.

I desire nothing apart from your good and perfect plan for my life. Thank you, dear Lord, for the safe harbor in which I dwell; you have given me peace I have never known. I thank you now for every day that I am blessed to walk with you.

"Oh, that men would give thanks to the LORD for His goodness, And for His wonderful works to the children of men!" (Psalm 107:15).

Thank you for being a God of new beginnings. Your love has replaced the fear that once consumed me with a foundation built on your holiness, and daily, the cornerstone of your strength fills me with a deep and growing confidence.

You have brought about a life-changing renewal to my mind, body, and spirit. You offer redemption from sin and the love offering of being in your presence throughout eternity. Nothing could bring greater joy. There is no question of your love for me, and in all heaven and earth, there is none like you.

"I will praise the LORD according to His righteousness, And will sing praise to the name of the LORD Most High" (Psalm 7:17).

During times of both joy and sorrow, you are always near. Your love and mercy have touched the deepest parts of who I was, who I am, and who I will one day become.

With a thankful heart and a growing security in who I am in you, I will daily lay my cares at the foot of the cross, for you have promised to bring holy order to my life.

———

"As for me, I will call upon God, And the Lord shall save me" (Psalm 55:16).

*T*hank you for always making a place for me in the shelter of your protective wing. It fills me with joy to know that no matter what my transgression, you faithfully make a space for me.

Your love never tires of watching over me as you have provided me with daily safety and security without fail. If I but look to you, Lord, you eagerly wait to walk with me, talk with me, and show me not only your ways but your will for my life. Blessed be your name.

---

*"How precious is Your lovingkindness, O God!
Therefore the children of men put their trust under
the shadow of Your wings" (Psalm 36:7).*

*A*s I turn to you for guidance and direction, it is so comforting to know that you know every detail of my life and you love and accept me unconditionally. There is no secret place that can be concealed from your loving and watchful eye. To you, dear Savior, goes all the glory, for you are worthy of praise.

As I willingly put off that which is old and become a new creature in Christ, I thank you, Lord, for your undying love.

———

"For there is not a word on my tongue, But behold, O Lord, You know it altogether" (Psalm 139:4).

The unifying truth that I am a product of your love has been the unbreakable link connecting me to your redemptive grace. While invisible to my heart, it was tangible to my soul.

I have exhausted every ounce of strength in an attempt to find stability and purpose while allowing so many to define me by what they saw outwardly.

You looked past the veneer of my polished composure and right straight through to my broken and missing pieces. You saw the soul wounds I hid from the world. You heard my cries and felt my fear.

You have vindicated me in my trouble, not by your sword, but through the cross. You have offered me healing and hope and a life with blessing and meaning. No longer do I hide behind a veneer. I am confident in not who I am, but whose I am.

What was hidden even from my own eyes is now because of your grace brought into the light for your glory. You have saved me from adversity and the strongholds that held my heart captive!

---

*"They confronted me in the day of my calamity,
But the Lord was my support" (Psalm 18:18).*

ecause of your never-ending compassion, you have given my life hope. Glory to you, Father, for your faithfulness. Thank you for never giving up on me. In my spirit, I pray my life will bring you glory and my actions will honor you, for you are worthy of praise. You have delivered me from darkness, and through your power, I have received healing and strength. Once I was weakened by fear, but I now stand confident as a child of the King.

Glory be to God; you are my living fortress.

---

*"Then they cried out to the LORD in their trouble,
And He delivered them out of their distresses"
(Psalm 107:6).*

ere words cannot express the joy and appreciation that warms the heart that has been touched by God. It is through your mercy, O Lord, that lives are changed and healing takes place. Thank you for daily washing away the pain and suffering and offering hope and light where only darkness has dwelled. To walk with you, Father, means restoration from brokenness and emptiness. Through you, it is possible to not just survive life but to live it abundantly.

"Oh, that men would give thanks to the LORD for His goodness, And for His wonderful works to the children of men!" (Psalm 107:21).

In heaven and earth, there is but one thing that can be put to the test and prevail. It is the Lord's Word. Lord, you have promised that no matter the situation or the hour, you are waiting for me to call on your name. Your touch calms the raging seas of my mind and brings me to a place of peace.

With my heart and mind centered on your love and goodness, I find rest. Savior, you are my all and all!

"But know that the LORD has set apart for Himself him who is godly; The LORD will hear when I call to Him" (Psalm 4:3).

*I*n you, I find the unconditional love of a father. In your presence, no threat can reach me. To daily experience your love and mercy creates in me a new and peaceful soul. With you at my side, I can rest easy knowing that you are my protector and my best interest is always your highest priority.

Lord, you want only for my life to be full of your good works, so with my eyes firmly fixed on you, my path will remain straight and sure. No harm can come to me; I have no worries of being overtaken by the enemy, for you are forever watching over me.

"In God (I will praise His word), In the LORD (I will praise His word), In God I have put my trust; I will not be afraid. What can man do to me?" (Psalm 56:10–11).

our touch brings instant relief; my heart flows with peace as the presence of your Spirit washes over me. Disaster cannot prevail under your power and glory, and I will fear not as you are with me always.

No harm can reach me; nor through your love and mercy can fear defeat me. I thank you, Lord, for always watching over me and daily placing my feet on solid ground. You are my Rock and my Deliverer.

"Then they cried out to the LORD in their trouble, And He saved them out of their distresses" (Psalm 107:13).

*A*s you continue daily to heal my brokenness and to fill my life with the blessing of your love, I pray you would fill my heart with a desire to worship only you. Father, I lay my life at your feet, in hopes that you would use me to help others and to bring glory and honor to your holy name.

Lord, in you alone I place my trust.

"Oh, fear the LORD, you His saints! There is no want to those who fear Him" (Psalm 34:9).

I wake to find that you have once again replaced the fear in my heart with a hymn of rejoicing. As the peace grows within me, I begin each day with my thoughts on you and your goodness. Your love for me shows no limits for you faithfully supply all of my needs in abundance. No longer do man-made dwellings offer me security, but every day that security is a gift from you.

No other is able to express the unconditional love that I have found in you, dear Lord. Thank you that minute by minute, hour by hour, and day by day, whatever my need is, you are always my faithful Creator, and never do you abandon your purpose for my life.

"The LORD is my strength and my shield; My heart trusted in Him, and I am helped; Therefore my heart greatly rejoices, And with my song I will praise Him" (Psalm 28:7).

You are the beacon that lights my path. It is beneath the comfort of your wing that offers me rest and where my spirit is renewed. I trust in your protection, for you have watched over me throughout my life and even before, in my mother's womb.

I thank you for your tender care and eternal pledge of love through Jesus Christ my Lord.

"But as for me, my prayer is to You, O Lord, in the acceptable time; O God, in the multitude of Your mercy, Hear me in the truth of Your salvation" (Psalm 69:13).

*T*hank you as you deliver me daily from anxiety and fear. Your blessings are too numerous to count, and through your mercy, I am able to walk in confidence because I have learned to put my trust in you and your commitment to me.

"Salvation belongs to the LORD. Your blessing is upon Your people. Selah" (Psalm 3:8).

Father, out of your great love for me, you have taken the weight of my burdens, making my load light. You are forever my strength and my shield. Daily you have been my comforter and my source of strength.

Without you, I would surely crumble under the weight of my fears, but you have delivered me out of darkness and given me a joyous heart and the hope of a new life in your glory. Praise your holy name.

"Blessed be the Lord, Who daily loads us with benefits, The God of our salvation! Selah" (Psalm 68:19).

*P*raise your holy name for your righteousness and faithfulness. Your love surpasses any that I have ever known. As I seek your name and daily surrender to your will, it is my prayer that you would reconstruct my life and wash away the pain and brokenness in my heart.

Lord, you are the master carpenter. I pray that you would make my heart and spirit into your likeness.

———

"Righteousness and justice are the foundation of Your throne; Mercy and truth go before Your face" (Psalm 89:14).

hroughout the greatest experiences of my life, the one thing I am always sure of is your presence. You are the comfort within me when my heart is full of sadness and the song when my soul rejoices. You are with me when my heart is filled with peace and are there to protect and soothe me when it is full of fear.

You are the rock in my life and my anchor in any storm. I praise you, Lord, and give thanks to you for never leaving me to flounder, for wherever I am, you are also there.

Praise be the name of the Lord my God.

"If I ascend into heaven, You are there; If I make my bed in hell, behold, You are there" (Psalm 139:8).

*D*aily your profound and uncompromised truth releases me from the snares of my captivity. I am in awe of your faithfulness and your commitment to me.

Lord, your healing knows no limits; nor is it bound by the limits of man's mind. Your love is so much more than I could have ever imagined. Knowing you are but a whisper away fills my mind with peace and my heart with a renewing love for you, sweet Savior.

"For the Lᴏʀᴅ hears the poor, And does not despise His prisoners" (Psalm 69:33).

During the times of my life when I have been too afraid to draw a breath, my deep and abiding faith in you always takes me to a place of peace and security. Your love and protection are my eternal refuge.

Thank you, Father, that my fear keeps me close to you and my spirit will always find rest in your presence. Praise you, dear Lord, for your ordinances and the life that springs forth from them.

———————

"The fear of the LORD is clean, enduring forever;
The judgments of the LORD are true and righteous
altogether" (Psalm 19:9).

You are the Alpha and the Omega, the beginning of all things and the end of things to come. It is a source of comfort and joy for those who suffer to know that you are the author and giver of life, and only through you can man's journey truly find a heavenly destiny.

You know the sin in man's heart, and the pain and suffering that he causes through his selfish and evil desires can only be made right by you. It is because you are God and once walked among us that we know you understand man's need and are able to heal and comfort those who seek your saving grace.

"Before the mountains were brought forth, Or ever You had formed the earth and the world, Even from everlasting to everlasting, You are God" (Psalm 90:2).

*Y*ou are the one true living God! You lavish love and guidance on your children. Grateful is my heart through the power of your spirit for a life centered in your will, a life that offers the blessing of eternal fellowship with you, our heavenly Creator.

Thank you for your daily love and protection. Father, you are my rock and my only source of lasting hope.

"The LORD lives! Blessed be my Rock! Let the God of my salvation be exalted" (Psalm 18:46).

ut of your love for me, you have kept your promise to take on the weight of my yoke and to make my burdens light enough that I am able to bear them.

As I learn to place my worries at your feet, you are faithful to deepen my trust in the power of your love. Help me to see that there is no fear in Christ Jesus, and with you for me, what can man do to harm me? Today I will sing praises to your name.

"In God (I will praise His word), In God I have put my trust; I will not fear. What can flesh do to me?" (Psalm 56:4).

From on high you have stood watch over me, desiring in your mercy that prosperity should evolve from your sacrifice. Your great love holds me to my course, my own unique journey, as I follow the path you have prepared and laid before me. I thank you for never losing sight of me. In my deepest hour of despair, you are always near and ready to comfort me, taking every opportunity captive to restore that which man has stolen by daily restoring peace to my fearful soul.

"He sent from above, He took me; He drew me out of many waters" (Psalm 18:16).

At times, anxiety becomes like a vast canyon. It overwhelms me as it consumes my every thought. In the midst of my fear, it is your face I seek. I look to you as the anxiety begins to fill my mind, and I whisper your name and wait for you to wash away the darkness with the promise of your Word. I can rest assured that you will rescue me because you are a faithful and loving Father. I can depend on you to lift me to safety and replace my fear and sadness with joy, which springs from your eternal love.

———

"You are my hiding place; You shall preserve me from trouble; You shall surround me with songs of deliverance. Selah" (Psalm 32:7).

I will rejoice for all eternity in the knowledge I was made to fellowship and walk with you in heaven's garden. Your love and devotion bring life to my spirit and fullness where there was once only emptiness.

As the you in me becomes more visible, I can't help but draw nearer to you and bask in the warmth of your love. Thank you for creating me.

"Your kingdom is an everlasting kingdom, And Your dominion endures throughout all generations" (Psalm 145:13).

I watch in awe as you stretch out your hand and touch my life. As I seek you, my life changes daily. I stand on the power of your endless love!

Before I knew you, I was filled with fear, but you have brought beauty and love into my life. I pray that I would see things through your eyes and that my every thought, action, and word would bring you glory and honor. Praise be the name of the Lord our God.

———

"I will praise You, for I am fearfully and wonderfully made; Marvelous are Your works, And that my soul knows very well" (Psalm 139:14).

ou are the author and provider of everything that is holy and good in my life. Aside from you, my efforts have been fruitless and in vain and have only resulted in more unhappiness and isolation from you, the only true source of comfort and healing.

———————

"Thank you, Father, for your promise to never leave of depart from me. My soul, wait silently for God alone, For my expectation is from Him" (Psalm 62:5).

*Y*ou are my shelter. As a child of the King, I can withstand any storm. I have faith that in hearing your name, my enemies will flee. I trust in you and rest assured because your love protects me, and at night I sleep in peace, knowing that you are watching over me.

With thanksgiving in my heart, I thank you for taking the terror out of the night by bringing light to the darkness within.

"You shall not be afraid of the terror by night, Nor of the arrow that flies by day" (Psalm 91:5).

You are the guiding force in my life. Through every leg of my journey, you have been there, and because of your infinite mercy, I can choose a new life filled with hope, security, and the assurance of your eternal presence.

I was lost, but because of your unconditional love, I now seek your face. The storms within must flee! No threat can prevail against your name. You are my sanctuary; where I am, you are also.

———

"But the salvation of the righteous is from the LORD; He is their strength in the time of trouble" *(Psalm 37:39).*

*Y*ou are the Creator of all living things, so I put my hope and faith in your caring hands; my security rests at your feet. Your sacrifice has been the supreme evidence of a father's love. Your amazing devotion to your children is all I need.

Please, dear Lord, let no one put your devotion to the test. Many experience harm at the hands of the ungodly. Let your mercy rest upon them as they wait for their deliverance. Let them take heart in knowing your peace, which surpasses all human understanding. Blessed be the name of the Lord, who is worthy of praise and honor.

———

"'For the oppression of the poor, for the sighing of the needy, Now I will arise,' says the LORD; "I will set him in the safety for which he yearns"' (Psalm 12:5).

As life's circumstances begin to rise up against me and rob me of the peace your spirit instills within me, let the truth of your Word reign supreme. Through your living Word, may mercy and truth guide and protect me from worldly influence.

Through prayer and meditation, your love fills my heart and restores the peace in my life. My existence is to fellowship with you, and I long to spend eternity in your presence.

"Do not withhold Your tender mercies from me, O Lord; Let Your lovingkindness and Your truth continually preserve me" (Psalm 40:11).

*E*very minute of every day, your love surrounds me with the glory of your compassion. My heart, which was once lost to the despair of shame and fear, now is redeemed in your presence, loved and fully accepted.

You have surrounded me with your tender mercy, which restored strength to my thirsty soul and gave peace to my wounded spirit.

———

"You shall increase my greatness, And comfort me on every side" (Psalm 71:21).

*T*hank you for teaching me through anxious moments that the only circumstance deserving of fear is being separated from you. Your love and mercy are a continual reminder of how faithful and righteous you are.

Daily, as I learn to place my trust in you, gratefulness fills my heart. I meditate on your scriptures and the many promises you have provided to remind me of my value and the spiritual prosperity that I have available as a child of the King.

"But the mercy of the LORD is from everlasting to everlasting On those who fear Him, And His righteousness to children's children" (Psalm 103:17).

When the enemy pursues me, my inner strengths and abilities are of no value. It is you, Lord, the keeper of my armor, who guards my life and restores peace in the midst of battle. Without you to save me, I would surely have perished.

At the whisper of your name, my enemies fall. Your love and protection are the foundation that together you and I are building my life. Through a relationship with you, I have found security and the faithful counsel I have desperately needed.

———————

"Give us help from trouble, For the help of man is useless" (Psalm 108:12).

aily your love and faithfulness give me the strength to stand strong in the face of fear and anxiety. Your endurance is a model of how to be steadfast and wait on the Father whose timing is perfect in all things.

Through your perfect love, my life is being healed, and my past is no more than fleeting reminders of the time before my heart responded to your call. I stand in your presence with incredible joy, embracing the opportunities you provide to pursue the purpose in which you created me for.

How can even a past life filled with torment overshadow the abundance of love and grace that befalls resting in the presence of the living God.

---

*"For His merciful kindness is great toward us,
And the truth of the LORD endures forever. Praise
the LORD!" (Psalm 117:2).*

*Y*our power is more than my mind can conceive! I look around me at the beauty you have created from a simple wave of your hand, and I have no doubt that you can heal the brokenness within my life, which creates such fear and anxieties.

I trust in your love, and I know that your passion for me is more intense than any emotion I could ever feel. By your request, I give you my fears, and you will take my yoke upon your shoulders, making my burdens light.

As I move forward day by day with you, Father, I trust in the amazing power of your endless love.

"He causes the vapors to ascend from the ends of the earth; He makes lightning for the rain; He brings the wind out of His treasuries" (Psalm 135:7).

*T*hank you for the peace of mind I find through spending time with you. When my thoughts race with anxiousness and worry consumes me, your Word is the food that sustains me. As you faithfully lift the chains of bondage and oppression from around me, I begin to experience the love of God and the peace that surpasses all worldly understanding.

Help me, Father, to continue to focus on you through prayer and meditation. May my life become daily transformed by the renewing of my mind and set my spirit set free.

"*Who executes justice for the oppressed, Who gives food to the hungry. The LORD gives freedom to the prisoners*" (*Psalm 146:7*).

*E*ven before the day of my birth, my life had purpose. As a child of the King, I only have to call upon the name of Jesus, and the glory of your love will outshine my fears.

By your will, I was created not to live in darkness, but to soar to heights beyond my wildest dreams. You are the Creator of heaven and earth, and in your holy name, I claim victory over the broken areas of my heart and declare that your glory will shine through the seasons of my life.

"For You formed my inward parts; You covered me in my mother's womb" (Psalm 139:13).

aily, through the power of your Word, my pain is being healed. Where I was once broken, I am now learning to trust in your amazing grace. As time goes by, you are giving me closure over the things that once held me in bondage and fear. I thank you, Lord, that in the midst of my pain you are closer than any friend.

I know that praying for your will and following your guidance is the key to my healing and to one day standing whole and restored.

"For He spoke, and it was done; He commanded, and it stood fast" (Psalm 33:9).

*K*nowing that you are never more than a whisper away gives me strength and comfort as I face the valleys in my life. Your ways are both amazing and righteous; nothing can compare to your love for me.

Oh, to be called a child of God is a wonderful thing. I thank you, Father, that no matter what trials or tribulations I face, I know I am not alone, that you will be with me, always directing my path.

"Deliver me in Your righteousness, and cause me to escape; Incline Your ear to me, and save me" (Psalm 71:2).

*I*n the storms, I look to you, for you are my safe place. I can trust in your faithfulness because you have promised to never leave or depart from me, and with you for me, nothing can come against me and be victorious.

Thank you, Father, that daily your love for me restores the broken places in my heart to a wholeness that I long to use to serve your kingdom.

"I have become as a wonder to many, But You are my strong refuge" (Psalm 71:7).

*E*ven when I have been unable to forgive myself, it gives me peace to know that you have forgiven me. Your blood covers every thought and every deed.

As a child of the King, there is nothing I should fear. With your hand on my life, my days can only follow your good and perfect will. Thank you, dear Lord, for your infinite mercy.

———

"But there is forgiveness with You, That You may be feared" (Psalm 130:4).

Your love brings soothing comfort to the broken places deep within my spirit. Daily as you touch my wounds, there is a growing desire in my heart to surrender my life completely to your will and divine purpose for my life.

"He heals the brokenhearted and binds up their wounds" (Psalm 147:3).

*A*s I read your words and meditate on your holiness, there is victory over the fear and anxiety that strives to control my thoughts and thwart the plans you have for my life. Father, I need a fresh revelation in this dark valley. Return my heart to a love of all that honors you!

I thank you for being a God who has been present in times of need as well as times of plenty. With a grateful heart, I rejoice over the good works that you will rise from the ashes of my past.

Please, Lord, come now and heal the sick and broken places in my mind, body, and soul. Restore the places in my heart wounded by life. Glory to you! In confidence, I stand knowing that you are far greater than any adversary I may face, have faced, or will face in the future. In Jesus's holy name, Amen!

———

"His heart is established; He will not be afraid, Until he sees his desire upon his enemies" (Psalm 112:8).

Daily as I spend time with you, I am always surprised by how your love touches and flows through my life, slowly and steadily transforming my spirit. Your greatness enriches my life and fills me with the ability to share that love with others. I pray that my life is a living testament to the life-changing love of Jesus.

"Praise Him for His mighty acts; Praise Him according to His excellent greatness!" (Psalm 150:2).

hank you that in the midst of my every circumstance, you hear my cries for help. It fills my heart with peace to know that you are with me. When others fall short, I can always count on you. It gives me tremendous peace and fills my heart with gladness to know that you love and care about every single area of my life.

"I cried to the LORD with my voice, And He heard me from His holy hill. Selah" (Psalm 3:4).

*I*n the midst of my fear and anxieties, I meditate on the truth of your Word and your desires for my life. How amazing you are, Father, to break the bondage of fear and shine like the dawn.

Help me to live out the days of my life according to your Holy Word and to walk in the path of your loving righteousness. Lord, make it the desire of my heart to turn away from the painful memories of my past and focus on all that is holy.

Father, you are the maker of everything good, and through my daily walk with you, I desire a spirit of humility that I may place my complete trust in you and encourage others to seek your face during times of pain and suffering. It is your healing touch that transforms lives.

"Commit your way to the LORD, Trust also in Him, And He shall bring it to pass. He shall bring forth your righteousness as the light, And your justice as the noonday" (Psalm 37:5–6).

hank you for loving me. I was lost, but you found me and delivered me from my world of fear. You delivered me out of the evil and sin that dwells within each of us. It is death to dwell in darkness apart from your wonderful Holy Spirit. You are the light of the world, and it is beside you that I desire to walk as you teach me of your ways.

Father, each day as you reveal yourself to me, the blinders created by my past are slowly lifted, and I feel your healing touch work its wonder all through my life. Your protection and care are all I need, for in you I have found a life with only peace and acceptance.

"You who love the LORD, hate evil! He preserves the souls of His saints; He delivers them out of the hand of the wicked" (Psalm 97:10).

*H*ow amazing it is to know that there are no limits on your love for me. Lord, to be your child, a sheep in your pasture resting peacefully in the shelter of your watchful eye, fills me with incredible peace, for no harm can come to me here in the safety of your love.

Prayerfully, I ask that every day I would come to know of your love and your will for my life in a more intimate and personal way and that I would see the world around me through your loving eyes. Thank you for creating me and calling me to be your child. You are my heavenly Father, and I love you more with each passing day.

—————

"Know that the LORD, He is God; It is He who has made us, and not we ourselves; We are His people and the sheep of His pasture" (Psalm 100:3).

ou are my fortress, in you and only in you have I found a sanctuary from the despair that was my life. No person, place, or thing can offer me the peace of mind and spirit I have found in you.

Thank you, Father, for claiming me as your own. There is nothing for me aside from your good and perfect will. In you, I have no worries and no fears, only peace and contentment.

> "To declare that the LORD is upright; He is my rock, and there is no unrighteousness in Him" (Psalm 92:15).

From the wellspring of your holiness, I am nourished with a daily diet of love and mercy. You have faithfully redeemed me and set my foot on higher ground times too numerous to count, when I have thought my best to have been a grander plan than the unknown design of yours.

Long before I acknowledged you as my Lord and Savior, you were my heavenly protector. Many times during my life, I have felt the power of your love go before me, blanketing me in safety as you sheltered me from a storm. Thank you, Father, for loving me so much that it has overcome the darkness in my soul.

"If I say, 'My foot slips,' Your mercy, O Lord, will hold me up" (Psalm 94:18).

I have searched my whole life for acceptance, and in you I have found a holy and relentless love that tells me I am safe. Your love provides a place, where I am free to trust, for there is no fear in Christ Jesus.

During my life, I have faced many trials, and you have been my safe refuge, a harbor that is full of peace and beauty, where I can rest. It would satisfy the deepest desires of my heart if I were to live a long life, speaking only of your goodness and mercies.

———

"But it is good for me to draw near to God; I have put my trust in the Lord God, That I may declare all Your works" (Psalm 73:28).

Fill my mind with the desire to meditate on your inspired Word and to sit quietly in your presence. As you renew my mind, help me to lean not on my own understanding, but to place my trust in you, the God who drives all out all fear and anxieties.

Lord, as I think upon the generosity of your love and devotion, it fills my heart with the deepest joy and causes my spirit to rejoice and sing praises to your holy name. I walk daily in the blessing of the risen Lamb.

"I will also meditate on all Your work, And talk of Your deeds" (Psalm 77:12).

I am praising your holy name! It is through your saving grace that I have found the peace that you alone provide. Lord, each morning you place gratefulness in my heart. Each night as you offer peace through the assurance of truth that, as I sleep, you will stand firm to your promises of provision, I sleep soundly knowing that you have assigned your heavenly angels to protect me while I rest. I pray that all the days of my life will be spent learning of the unconditional and sacrificial love of God.

Daily I seek to dwell with you in peace, honoring you with my every breath. Show me, heavenly Father, what I can do to share your love that flows through me. It is my desire to humbly wait upon your direction. Use me, Lord!

Thank you, Father, for hearing my cry and rescuing me from my oppressor.

"Lord, You have heard the desire of the humble; You will prepare their heart; You will cause Your ear to hear; To do justice to the fatherless and the oppressed, That the man of the earth may oppress no more" (Psalm 10:17–18).

*U*nmoved by the storms that have wreaked havoc on my life in endless nights, I have cried out to you. How great is my God as you deliver me from my torment! Ministering angels are swiftly dispatched to comfort me as you respond to my desperate need for deliverance.

My portion never lacks my Father's devoted love!

I know as sure as my need will arise that you are already in that moment, ready to cast down any evil that dare come against me. Your Word is my guiding light, one forged in the indestructible and undeniable blood of Jesus!

Show me, Lord, how to reach the darkness with your light that shines from my heart to offer help and encouragement to those seeking the protection of the eternal fortress.

"The LORD of hosts is with us; The God of Jacob is our refuge. Selah" (Psalm 46:7).

The joy of knowing I will be with you in heaven fills my heart with abiding peace. The burdens of the world are light when daily my focus is on your kingdom.

I trust in your Word and know that your promises are formed out of perfect love, which drives away all my anxieties. Praising you in the highest, I will shout your name from the mountaintops.

"But I have trusted in Your mercy; My heart shall rejoice in Your salvation" (Psalm 13:5).

*T*hank you for your love and acceptance, even when those around me judge my deeds harshly. You never forsake me!

In you, I have the promise of truth and love. As I seek your will for my life, I find daily reassurance through your living Word that you will never fall short. Your love is complete, and it casts out all fears.

———————

"When my father and my mother forsake me,
Then the LORD will take care of me" (Psalm 27:10).

*Y*ou supply me with strength when I am weak and with shelter when I am afraid. Your love restores my spirit and comforts me during the storms of my life.

When fear closes in and anxious thoughts begin to rush through my mind, I know you are only a whisper away. Thank you, Father, for your eternal mercy and your undying love for me.

"The Lord is their strength, And He is the saving refuge of His anointed" (Psalm 28:8).

avior, there is none like you in all the earth. Your throne is on high, yet you inhabit my heart. You sit at the right hand of God, and yet you dwell in the midst of my worry and fear. Your character is abundant with love and mercy as you rush to reside within all who seek you.

None can compare to the majestic way you watch me from your throne knowing all I do. Your care and provision provide me with shelter and fills me with peace.

Without you, emptiness and despair would be my hope. I am so thankful that my life is your great treasure. You are my Redeemer, my Father, my Confidant, and the Deliverer of my soul.

---

*"Who is like the L*O*RD our God, Who dwells on high" (Psalm 113:5).*

When danger lurks and my peace fades, it is not by my will but your compassion that is vast beyond the limitless universe, which soothes and reinforces the bond we share.

I call out to you, Lord, "Help me!" You hear my cry, and I know you are with me through the confirming presence of your peace, a sacred occurrence beyond my human understanding.

Blessed am I that your benevolent nature never abandons the sound of my voice. With my thoughts refocused, I know my gaze must stay fixed on my deliverer, the One who is my safe harbor and my eternal home!

"Not unto us, O LORD, not unto us, But to Your name give glory, Because of Your mercy, Because of Your truth" (Psalm 115:1).

Your love is pure, and with it, you heal hearts and change lives. Your tender arms have lifted me out of the valley of death, exposing one set of footprints as you carried me. You have placed my feet on the path of eternal righteousness.

Basking in the warmth of your light, surely nothing can surpass the assurance of the hope that is in you. My heart fully surrenders to your steadfast promises to daily assume my burdens along with my joys.

I am in awe of your never-ending capacity to renew what the enemy meant for evil. Lord, that I would love what you love and seek what you alone have to offer.

"The Lord opens the eyes of the blind; The Lord raises those who are bowed down; The Lord loves the righteous" (Psalm 146:8).

Thank you, Father, that I may come freely and boldly to the altar and cast down all that has been placed on my heart by the One who knows. Such peace is found in knowing not who I am but whose I am. Ah! That the Creator of the universe dwells within me. Praise!

My heart dances with anticipation as I share with you the deep longings of my soul. With your ear inclined, I utter requests for the lost, the sick, and those in need, affirmed in your Word that each is more precious to you than gold.

Each day offers new hope as I lay my petitions before the throne! You are a generous God with endless reservoirs of love and compassion, offering eternal life to those who would but choose to walk with you. Lord, I will serve you joyfully all the days of my life.

———

"My voice You shall hear in the morning, O LORD; In the morning I will direct it to You, And I will look up" (Psalm 5:3).

*I*n this ever-changing world, where darkness seems to prevail, shadowing sovereign rule, the King of Kings brings light and life, driving back the lies of hopelessness and despair that foster anxious and fearful thinking.

Lord, you are the breath of life, faithful to deliver me from the enemy's plan to rob, kill, and destroy your chosen. The devil's divisive narrative is no match for the holy refuge of the Master. No stronghold can withstand the prayers of the saints who are in Christ Jesus. Blessed by the name of the Lord God.

"The Lord also will be a refuge for the oppressed,
A refuge in times of trouble" (Psalm 9:9).

*F*ather, I was knit together in your image and by design, complete only through your love. The holy shield that surrounds me provides shelter where I safely surrender to the River of Life, which gives hope to my once-bankrupt soul.

Thank you for the hedge of protection that surrounds me as I follow you along the unique path, which you designed for me before the beginning of time. As you teach me to live a fearless and abundant life, exposing me to new truths that cause my spirit to soar, I beseech you to provide fellow travelers that I might bless, as I have been abundantly blessed.

Your perfect will is a living testament of your grace. Shine your light and continue to expose the plans that are disguised to prosper a man's soul while guiding him into the darkness that I would see the world through your eyes, Lord, and, along with the saints, burden-share for all of creation still making their way through the wilderness to partake in your grace.

"Show me Your ways, O Lord; Teach me Your paths" (Psalm 25:4).

*Y*ou are the truth that races in to guard my mind when the enemy's attacks cause me to retreat in anguish. Because of the completeness of your redeeming love, I am restored, a new creation!

By reaching into the pit and pulling your Lamb to safety, you have provided hope when all in my life seemed hopeless!

Allow me, Lord, through your fullness to run the sanctifying race you have placed before me. Teach me to press into eternal opportunities, loving those whom you love and caring for the least. With all of eternity before me, I bend my knee to the Way Maker!

———

"Into Your hand I commit my spirit; You have redeemed me, O LORD God of truth" (Psalm 31:5).

No other god I have pursued has given me strength when I was weak or peace when I was overcome with fear. Only you, Jesus! Blessed be the tribulation that causes hearts to open to the only source of eternal life.

Thank you, Lord, for filling my heart with hope where fear once dominated. At a time when your voice seemed distant, you shined the light of truth that it was I who sought refuge and comfort from idols. Praise your holy name for hearing the longing and despair within me to be filled from the holy haven of your spirit.

My King! You are the only One who is faithful and worthy of worship and praise. Guide my steps to share your love with those who are in need of the eternal rock!

"From the end of the earth I will cry to You, When my heart is overwhelmed; Lead me to the rock that is higher than I" (Psalm 61:2).

*P*lease, Lord! From within your overflowing storehouse, fill my cup with love that I might cross the dessert of trepidation and journey into the meadow of your ever-lasting grace. All the days of my life I will sing praises to you for placing fertile soil in my heart and solid ground beneath my feet.

Your blood was shed for all, yet many refuse to receive that which they cannot see. Their gift is free and set aside for them by the living God!

Use me, Lord, that I might be a witness to the blessings and goodness that follow those whose heart belongs to the Lord God Almighty.

"I am the Lord your God, Who brought you out of the land of Egypt; Open your mouth wide, and I will fill it" (Psalm 81:10).

*T*he works of your hands are remarkable, ushering the highest good into my life. Daily I rejoice in the blessing it is to be your child. You are my Lord, my God, and my Creator; none can compare in this complicated world to the simplicity and beauty of your sacrificial love.

Your love runs deep, covering my past, present, and future with merciful grace. In you, I have found healing from my brokenness. You are the Redeemer of my soul and the guide to my spirit.

Your love is infinitely greater than I have ever experienced; my faith has been built through your protection and nurturing. Bless the LORD, O my soul!

"O LORD my God, You are very great: You are clothed with honor and majesty" (Psalm 104:1).

*L*ord, your shield of faith protects me when the marquee playing in my mind has persistent images that leave behind an intrusive emotional layer. These disturbing feelings force me to search for the author of my fear. The search is short! The enemy's perpetual mission to destroy your children is not new; nor are his tactics.

Thank you, Father, for faithfully watching for questioning that the weight of life is too heavy for me. You are faithful! I pray that you would create in me an unwavering spirit that I would be steadfast in my walk with you. Your blessings are abundant, and your peace has given my heart strength.

Give me discernment that I may never miss the opportunities you put before me to help those in need. I trust in you, my Savior, for you alone are worthy of worship.

"He will not be afraid of evil tidings; His heart is steadfast, trusting in the LORD" (Psalm 112:7).

My worth comes from the precious value you have placed in me. I am so thankful that you are faithful and committed to restoring my life. It is my desire to serve you with a heart of gratitude and a spirit of submission.

Heavenly Father, as you continue to watch over me, I pray for truth to forge a deep vein of love between us. You have sustained me when the full weight of hopelessness has left me crippled. In love, you sent your Spirit into the secret places of my heart, transforming the darkness with your holy presence.

In you, I have been made whole and returned to the full measure of my height. I have learned to rejoice for surely you have spared me from the death and isolation of a life without your eternal vow of love.

Father, let your Word make my heart impatient to surrender to the promises you have made to honor and rescue me in times of trouble. Advance my pace at the opportunity to share the hope I have found in you, Lord Jesus.

"The LORD upholds all who fall,, And raises up all who are bowed down" (Psalm 145:14).

You have shown me the greatest of favor by devastating the plans the enemy had years ago, placed well in motion to crush the complete worth of my life. Your love has created in me a truth that can never be torn from me!

It is precious and holy to be an image-bearer of the Almighty Risen God! I will spend my days embracing the holy moments in your presence and the divine work you have set before me. My heart is filled with thanksgiving as I reflect on how you have transformed my life.

It is through your sanctifying love that I have something of eternal value to share with others, which I pray will lead them to the same favor that I have found to be in abundance. I love you, Father!

"Remember me, O Lord, with the favor You have toward Your people. Oh, visit me with Your salvation" (Psalm 106:4).

*L*ord, you are faithful to walk with me through the valley of my daily fears and anxieties; I depend on your covering of mercy and strength as I face down the strongholds created so many years ago, which have kept me from the fullness of whom you created me to be.

I extend my hand daily in victory and with longing for your touch to be filled with your embrace and fully occupied with your will. Thank you, Father, for inhabiting the praises of your people!

"I lay down and slept; I awoke, for the LORD sustained me" (Psalm 3:5).

My Response to 2020

As catastrophe becomes the new norm, each new day offers the endless potential for fear and anxiety. The enemy is relentless as he presses in, and with each blow, his attacks become more personal, causing chaos, conflict, and unthinkable suffering. My soul trembles! I pray that my faith would drive out my fears.

Father, as the enemy continues to wage war against the world, thwart his plans and turn his deeds back on him hundredfold. Unite the church to boldly, as one body of believers, go out and stand in the gap, becoming a bridge of hope while doing the work you have proclaimed, to spread the love of Jesus to every person, without regard to race, religion, color, or geography.

I declare today that I stand with you! Battle-ready to, along with the army of saints, fight this spiritual war, pushing back the darkness and allowing the light of Jesus to shine for every soul to behold. Turn this land and every country back to you that in blessing we could walk in peace.

"Be merciful to me, O God, be merciful to me! For my soul trusts in You; And in the shadow of Your wings I will make my refuge, Until these calamities have passed by" (Psalm 57:1).

Epilogue

I stood in the shadow of gardens filled with beauty and fragrance. For me, there was no hope for fragrance or dreams filled with blooms. I stood in the shadows, watching the parade of exquisitely arrayed pedals, adorned with grace and elegance.

I stood in the shadows, and with flowing tears, I asked the Creator of this magnificent garden, "Why was I in the shadows without fragrance and bloom?"

He answered back, "You are in the shadows by your own choosing."

He then allowed me for a moment to see myself through his eyes.

What I witnessed was a beautiful flower like no other in the garden. The flower I saw was rich with color, but it was also dying. This flower needed to be in the light, but thorns were clinging to the lovely flower, holding it captive, and rather than stepping away from the shade and the thorns, the flower was holding tightly to them.

The Lord told the beautiful flower that if it wanted to live, it only needed to let go of the past and step into the light. There, it would find life filled with fragrance and bloom.

"But I am poor and sorrowful; Let Your salvation, O God, set me up on high" (Psalm 69:29).

Printed in the United States
By Bookmasters